The Readers' Advisory Guide
to Street Literature

ALA READERS' ADVISORY SERIES

The Readers' Advisory Guide to Street Literature

Vanessa Irvin Morris

FOREWORD BY
Teri Woods

Joyce Saricks and Neal Wyatt
SERIES EDITORS

American Library Association
Chicago   2012

Vanessa Irvin Morris is an assistant professor at the College of Information Science and Technology at Drexel University, Philadelphia, Pennsylvania (the iSchool at Drexel). She has spent twenty years serving in academic, special, school media, and public libraries. Her research interests include the sociocultural anthropology of small, urban, and rural libraries, literacy practices of public service librarians, and literacy practices enacted and learned in Second Life. Morris founded and facilitated a teen book club focusing on street lit, working with inner-city teens at a Philadelphia library from 2005 to 2008. She is currently pursuing her EdD and is conducting her dissertation research on "Street Literature as Collaborative Inquiry for Urban Public Service Librarians" with the University of Pennsylvania Graduate School of Education.

Printed in the United States of America

16   15   14   13   12   5   4   3   2   1

While extensive effort has gone into ensuring the reliability of the information in this book, the publisher makes no warranty, express or implied, with respect to the material contained herein.

ISBNs: 978-0-8389-1110-5 (paper); 978-0-8389-9362-0 (PDF); 978-0-8389-9363-7 (ePUB); 978-0-8389-9364-4 (Mobipocket); 978-0-8389-9365-1 (Kindle). For more information on digital formats, visit the ALA Store at alastore.ala.org and select eEditions.

Library of Congress Cataloging-in-Publication Data

Morris, Vanessa Irvin.
     The readers' advisory guide to street literature / Vanessa Irvin Morris ; foreword by Teri Woods.
          p.   cm.
     Includes bibliographical references and index.
     ISBN 978-0-8389-1110-5 (alk. paper)
     1. Urban fiction, American—Bibliography. 2. Urban fiction, American—History and criticism. 3. Street life—Fiction—Bibliography. 4. Young adult fiction, American—Bibliography. 5. Readers' advisory services—United States. 6. Fiction in libraries.
     I. Title.
     Z1231.U73M67 2012
     [PS374.U73]
     016.813'609358209732—dc23   2011029685

Cover image © Hannamariah/Shutterstock, Inc.

⊗ This paper meets the requirements of ANSI/NISO Z39.48-1992 (Permanence of Paper).

ALA Editions purchases fund advocacy, awareness, and accreditation programs for library professionals worldwide.

To my ancestors and to my parents,
Roger and Barbara Irvin,
for consistently and beautifully modeling to me
the art of reading, writing, and honest hard work.

To Bernard Vavrek, Ph.D.,
and Helen Miller, MLS,
for believing in me early on and
starting me on my way.

CONTENTS

EPILOGUE

APPENDIX

SERIES INTRODUCTION

Joyce Saricks and Neal Wyatt
SERIES EDITORS

In a library world in which finding answers to readers' advisory questions is often considered among our most daunting service challenges, library staff need guides that are supportive, accessible, and immediately useful. The titles in this series are designed to be just that. They help advisors become familiar with fiction genres and nonfiction subjects, especially those they don't personally read. They provide ready-made lists of "need to know" elements such as key authors and read-alikes, as well as tips on how to keep up with trends and important new authors and titles.

Written by librarians with years of RA experience who are also enthusiasts of the genre or subject, the titles in this series of practical guides emphasize an appreciation of the topic, focusing on the elements and features fans enjoy, so advisors unfamiliar with the topics can readily appreciate why they are so popular.

Because this series values the fundamental concepts of readers' advisory work and its potential to serve readers, viewers, and listeners in whatever future-space libraries inhabit, the focus of each book is on appeal and how appeal crosses genre, subject, and format, especially to include audio and video as well as graphic novels. Thus, each guide emphasizes the importance of whole collection readers' advisory and explores ways to make suggestions that include novels, nonfiction, and multimedia, as well as how to incorporate whole collection elements into displays and booklists.

Each guide includes sections designed to help librarians in their RA duties, be that daily work or occasional interactions. Topics covered in each volume include:

> The appeal of the genre or subject and information on subgenres and types so that librarians might understand the breadth and scope of the topic and how it relates to other genres and subjects. A brief history is also included to give advisors context and highlight beloved classic titles.

Descriptions of key authors and titles with explanations of why they're important: why advisors should be familiar with them and why they should be kept in our collections. Lists of read-alikes accompany these core author and title lists, allowing advisors to move from identifying a key author to helping patrons find new authors to enjoy.

Information on how to conduct the RA conversation so that advisors can learn the tools and skills needed to develop deeper connections between their collections and their communities of readers, listeners, and viewers.

A crash course in the genre or subject designed to get staff up to speed. Turn to this section to get a quick overview of the genre or subject as well as a list of key authors and read-alikes.

Resources and techniques for keeping up to date and understanding new developments in the genre or subject are also provided. This section will not only aid staff already familiar with the genre or subject, but will also help those not familiar learn how to become so.

Tips for marketing collections and lists of resources and awards round out the tools staff need to be successful working with their community.

As readers who just happen to be readers' advisors, we hope that the guides in this series lead to longer to-be-read, -watched, and -listened-to piles. Our goal is that the series helps those new to RA feel supported and less at sea, and introduces new ideas or new ways of looking at foundational concepts, to advisors who have been at this a while. Most of all, we hope that this series helps advisors feel excited and eager to help patrons find their next great title. So dig in, explore, learn, and enjoy the almost alchemical process of connecting title and reader.

FOREWORD

Teri Woods

I was asked to write this foreword and my first thought was, "What will I say to the readers?" I think I would say to those of you already familiar with the street-lit genre, those of you who are big fans, those of you who have supported this movement, and those of you who understand the stories and know the characters and know what you're reading like the back of your hand, thank you. You need to know that you are the reason I am, and you are the reason I will continue to be. I'm such a small part of this movement as a writer, but you as a reader are ardent; thus, you are the reason street lit, or urban fiction as some call it, exists. If it were not for you, it would not be.

These street-lit books are representing a voice of what was never to be spoken or told. And it is a voice that you hear very well. Not everyone can hear the cries of the inner-city streets. Not everyone cares to understand the tears on a Black face and what they represent or how to make them go away. This new-wave genre of street lit will always remind the human race of a people who were supposed to be forgotten, swept under a rug, put in a box—better yet a cell—never to have a voice, never to cry out, and never able to speak out against the injustice we live in, see, experience in our everyday life just because of our demographics. Well, that's just not going to happen now, is it? No, it won't, because of all of you. I could write these books all day; it wouldn't make a difference if you didn't buy them. But you do, and I thank you.

I need you to know that from the first time I stepped outside with *True to the Game*, I was rejected. I had more people turn on me and talk with such dismay that it hindered my thinking, but it didn't stop my determination. I can count the number of people who said things to me like,

TERI WOODS is author of the classic work *True to the Game*. Self-published in 1999, *True to the Game* is a pioneering novel that helped ignite the twenty-first-century street-literature movement. Woods ultimately published *True to the Game* as a trilogy, with the second installation in the series, *True to the Game: Gena*, appearing on the New York Times Best-Seller List at the time of its publication, in November 2007. Woods is also author of the highly acclaimed Dutch trilogy, the novel *Alibi*, and other popular contemporary street-lit titles.

"Black people don't read. You're wasting your time." Then there were those who had worked very hard, I'm sure, and received a formal education who had their personal opinions. Many of them also said, "You can't write. That's not English. You don't even use proper grammar; you can't write these slang words in a book." And of course the backlash for having the "*N* word" on every page didn't help either.

There is a concept, a notion, that is pushed on us to believe that we are to speak and act a certain way to show respect and to be respected, and the *N* word is the token for that concept. My use of it in my writings of everyday street life shatters that notion, and to me personally, that notion is merely mythological or, better yet, an opinion, to say the least. Is there not freedom of speech, or is that freedom only provided as far as what an individual deems appropriate?

When it was all said and done, I don't think there was one person who believed in me or my writing, not one, in the beginning. No matter how big I am or how small I am, how rich I am or how poor I am, how high or how low I may be at times in my life, I will always be grateful to those who have supported me and to those who have supported that which I write.

I am positive that this journey of independent publishing and the books that I write, and the readership that supports them, speaks volumes to all those who said I would never sell a book and that I was wasting my time. If it doesn't, then the fact that I was able to slip through the cracks and sell a million books independently does, I'm sure. Either way, it doesn't have to speak to them, to those who are appalled and ashamed, I offer you silence—you'll get no apologies here. But moreover, I think my books and street lit in and of itself don't have to speak to everyone, don't have to appeal to everyone, don't have to be accepted by everyone. And that's OK, because I know that my books and street lit speak to us— between you, dear reader, and me, that's all that matters to me anyway. You are my readers, and the connection that I share with you through my mind and through our reading together is something that no one will ever be able to take from me or from you. That's the beauty of reading—the journey, the story, the plot, and the world in which it takes you—and that, for me, is what writing is all about. It's my job to take you somewhere far, far, far away, to another place and time, with characters who feel, and live, and breathe, and of course remind you of someone you may already know, even if that someone is yourself.

That's what I do, that's my job, and although my work focuses on the journey into inner-city life, turmoil, and street drama, I don't think it should matter much if the story is about inner-city streets or farmland, but rather the journey you take when reading a story. That's what writing and reading is about for me, the journey.

I have been told by so many librarians that the kids come into the library looking for my books, that for some I am the first book, the first journey on paper, that they have ever read in their lives. I am the first author to take them outside their own existence and into another world. And after exploring my world and reading my book, all the young readers want to take another journey, if not with me, then with another writer. They say the pen is mightier than the sword, and so, from reading street lit, the children become readers when before they didn't read anything.

Some people would say that the genre of street lit has no substance, that street lit is merely a fad and that the books and the authors won't be around after tomorrow. If that is the case, then I ask, Who will tell the stories tomorrow? Who will give voice to all the injustices of Black people so that we are not uncounted for? I truly, humbly, beg to differ with those nonbelievers. I'm still here twelve years later and counting, still writing and publishing street lit.

I don't think anyone can undo that which I have done as a pioneer in this genre because the voice of the people is now too loud. History has already been set in motion, the groundwork has already been laid, the blueprint has successfully been implemented, and Black and Latino folks are writing and telling their stories and selling them, transforming the lives of readers. I don't think I need to say much more to substantiate that which I do and that which I have done. It's too late to sweep street lit under the rug, and it's much too late to question its worth in the publishing industry.

To date, major publishers have recognized the income that self-published street-lit authors have generated. They are aware of the street hustle taking place with urban books and the millions of dollars we are independently generating. The hustle is good on the one hand and it's bad on the other, because we are talking about the people writing and self-publishing these street-lit stories making hundreds, thousands, and even millions of dollars. The publishers have also recognized the ongoing sales potential of street lit.

In the beginning, no one was paying attention to me and what started out as an independent publishing movement, my small Harriet Tubman, Underground Railroad way of selling books. Now major publishing houses are offering deals and signing street-lit authors in an attempt to control the millions of dollars that can be potentially earned from publishing street-lit novels. This takeover of street-lit publishing is the way it has been done for centuries, that is, simply business. And the street-lit business is huge.

Street lit encompasses hip-hop rappers like Snoop Dogg, 50 Cent, and Cash Money Millionaires. I believe that using big celebrity names is a way that the publishing industry tries to control the street-lit genre. The upside is that all those who frowned upon street lit will stop opinionating because they all want a piece of the street-lit pie, and I don't think anyone can possibly question me regarding street lit's worth from a financial standpoint. Filmmakers are already seeking street-lit books to be the next cash earners at the box office, and everyone is trying to get in on the action. Even daytime television is looking for stories containing street-lit material. It's a very exciting time, and it has been an exciting journey for me from the very beginning.

I have learned much from writing and self-publishing street lit. I have learned a lot from you, my readers, and from working with a major publishing house. I know that which I started has made me successful, but more important, that which I started hasn't made me forget who I am, a working-class girl from Philly and a former wifey who was living very dangerously. I was the wayward runaway teen who wanted to forget how I was raised and the strong family of women and men who raised me. I was that teen girl, but I did not forget.

So, I write for my father, my uncle, and my family who weren't allowed to go to school because they were made to pick cotton as small children. I write for my mother, born in 1930, during the Great Depression, and the struggles of her life. Her imprint, passed on to me from my ancestors, lives within me. I write for my brothers, who gave their lives to the streets for their families to have a better life and who are now resting behind bars. Their sacrifice has gone unnoticed for far too long.

I also write for mothers in the 'hood who lost it all when they lost their baby boys to the streets from being gunned down and murdered—tragically violent lives, gone forever. I write for all that I've seen, for all that I've done, for every place I've been, for every face I know, for eyes staring into mine, for hearts broken, for loves lost, for loves found, for birth, for pain, for death, for vain; I write for all that I believe, for all that I don't, for all I wish for, for all I want to know, for all the places I wish to go. I write for income, but I'll be poor before I write for those who misunderstand—and I write simply because I can.

In this book, *The Readers' Advisory Guide to Street Literature*, you, the reader, will learn more about what street lit is from a historical perspective, and you'll learn that reading is one of the most powerful things you could ever do for your own education and personal growth. Vanessa Irvin Morris has put together an important text that fully explains what street lit is and how you can enjoy the genre in many ways in the library by checking out the books (and returning them!), attending book clubs to discuss the books, meeting authors (like me) at library events, and talking with librarians and teachers to let them know what and who you want to read. Be a bold reader and tell them what you want. There is no shame in reading street lit; there is only shame in educators not being open to understanding it.

I realize that this book is mainly targeted to teachers and librarians so that you can learn how to best deal with this genre called street lit, or urban fiction, in the libraries and even in the classrooms. Because I write foremost for the readers of street lit, please understand that my voice in this foreword is for the readers you don't necessarily want to see reading street lit: the teen girl popping her gum while reading a street-lit novel at the Laundromat or hair salon, the young adult male sitting on the stoop in the 'hood while quietly reading a novel, the working-class woman reading a street-lit novel while on her way to work or home on the city train or bus, or the library patron who comes into your library wanting to know, "Where the Black books at?"

I'm here to say this: give them the book that lets them read. Trust that the power of reading is what is affecting readers the most, regardless of what you, as an educator, might deem appropriate. This readers' guide is an invaluable resource to help all of us to trust readers' own wisdom about what stories move them, inspire them, and entertain them. *The Readers' Advisory Guide to Street Literature* will educate you on what "the Black books" are in terms of the genre of street lit. I am honored to be able to support this endeavor, because I write "the Black books" to entertain the reader, and in turn, the reader is transformed. It's all good, and it is what it is. It's street lit.

—February 2010

ACKNOWLEDGMENTS

My daughters (in order of appearance): Jasmine, Amrita, Julia, Kahaja, and Tanisha. Thank you, ladies, for not freaking out when I visited your classrooms as the neighborhood librarian, for keeping your cool when I was a substitute teacher in your classes or the librarian at your schools or became friends with your teachers; thank you for being such avid readers and writers of not just text but also of life. Thank you for being the joys of my life.

My elders: my parents, Roger and Barbara Irvin, Pearl Womack Irvin, Roland Irvin, Deborah Irvin, Lillian Blango, Sandra Thompson. My women's village: my sisters, Vernita "Nee" Irvin and Monique "Moni" Thompson, and my cousins Oji "Toni" Dunia, Rochelle "Rodi" Irvin Aikens, and Donna Long. My village council: Gena Chambers MacKenzie, Selma "Sam" Williams, Jeff Bullard, Roberta "Berta" Jean Vengley, Fabian Joseph, Michelle Rogers, Amy Nadell, Angela Willie, Robin Osborne, Jameela Gage, Claudia Martinez, Biany Perez, Patrice Berry, Nirva LaFortune, Robin Naughton, Kinte McDaniel, Clare Bohn, and Jevon McDuffie.

University of Pennsylvania's Graduate School of Education (UPenn GSE): Susan Lytle, Ph.D.; Gerald Campano, Ph.D.; Lawrence Sipe, Ph.D. (1949–2011); the UPenn GSE Reading/Writing/Literacy program staff; and my cohort-colleagues Lynnette Harris-Scott; Esther Ra Park; Sarah Hobson; Christina Rose Dubb, Ph.D.; Maria Ghiso, Ph.D.; and Rob Simon, Ph.D. Also thank you to Christopher Crowley from the University of Wisconsin–Madison's School of Education; Marc Lamont Hill, Ph.D., from Teachers College at Columbia University; and Megan Sweeney, Ph.D., of the University of Michigan's Department of English Language and Literature.

The iSchool at Drexel (University): a wonderful place for me to be. Thank you to the entire administration, faculty, and staff—everyone—for your amazing support of my endeavors, especially Alison Lewis, Ph.D., and Kris Unsworth, Ph.D. I also thank Kristine Lewis, Ph.D., of Drexel's

School of Education, and I'd like to acknowledge the faculty and staff at the Department of Library Science at Clarion University of Pennsylvania.

Thank you to the following colleagues: Daniel Marcou, MLS, of Streetfiction.org; Wilda Williams, MLS, of *Library Journal*; Megan Honig, MLS, of *YALS: The Official Journal of the Young Adult Library Services Association*; Rory Litwin, MLS, and Isabel Espinal, MLS, of Library Juice Press; and Linda Duggins of Grand Central Publishing. Thank you to the following authors: Teri Woods, Zetta Elliott, K'wan Foye, Wahida Clark, Vickie Stringer, KaShamba Williams, Kenji Jasper, Terra Little, Kia Dupree, Relentless Aaron, and Ashley and JaQuavis Coleman.

A huge thank-you to the Widener Teen Street-Lit Book Club (2005–2008), and my deepest appreciation to all public service and school librarians—notably, the Pennsylvania African American Library Association's Librarian Book Club and the Westchester (NY) Library System's Librarian Book Club—as well as Bruce Siebers, Veronica Britto, Darren Cottman, Marvin DeBose, and Christina Holmes in Philadelphia; Rachee Fagg in Lansdowne, Pennsylvania; K. C. Boyd in Chicago; Susan McClelland in Evanston, Illinois; Edi Campbell in Indianapolis, Indiana; D. L. Grant in San Antonio, Texas; and my social media librarian friends and followers on Facebook, Second Life, and Twitter. Thank you for all that you do on the front lines; I am humbled by your practice.

INTRODUCTION

Two critical incidents happened to me that led me to write this book. One event occurred during my childhood and the other during my career as an adult and teen librarian.

The first incident occurred by virtue of my father having always been a prolific reader. Growing up as a bi-city (really, bi-'hood) kid in both 1970s Camden, New Jersey, and the northern part of Philadelphia (known as North Philly), I sat with my dad every Sunday as he read the Sunday newspaper. He'd be in his La-Z-Boy chair reading the news and sports sections of the *Philadelphia Inquirer*, and I'd be on the floor right beneath him reading the comics and playing word games. Every evening during the week, he brought home the *Philadelphia Daily News*, and I always saw him reading a book of some kind. It was he who introduced me to titles like *Manchild of the Promised Land* (1965), *The Autobiography of Malcolm X* (1965), and *The Honey Badger* (1965). My mother was an avid reader of the Bible and *The Upper Room* pamphlet. My paternal grandmother introduced me to my very first library collection: her three-shelf bookcase in the main hallway of her apartment, where she had books like *Robinson Crusoe* and Ian Fleming novels. Her library contained a lot of "guy books," which made sense for her because she had four sons. My grandmother also subscribed to *Reader's Digest* and kept the Bible by her bedside. My grandmother was also the first poet I ever met.

When I was about nine years old, my father knowing that I, too, liked to read, gave me a book of his, titled *Pimp* (1969), by Iceberg Slim. OK. So it wasn't exactly the kind of book you give to a nine-year-old. But my father knew that I was a smart kid with good grades who liked to read. So he trusted that I was also cognitively mature for my age. Perhaps he was right, perhaps he was not. Nevertheless, I began reading the book and was enthralled, fascinated, and openmouthed at what I was reading. This reading journey lasted about twenty-five pages, because my mother walked by and saw me reading it and promptly confiscated it from my hands, turned on her heels, and marched down the hallway, yelling, "Raj!" (short for Roger, my father's name).

So, that was event number one. Me—as a reader of street lit, my first exposure to the genre, circa 1974.

Fast-forward to my adulthood, when my love of reading evolved into a wonderful career as a librarian. I was very happy to be able to serve as a librarian in the same Philly neighborhood where I grew up: the Strawberry Mansion section of North Philadelphia.

The second event was my reintroduction to the street-lit genre during the summer of 2000. I was the adult and teen librarian at the Widener Branch Library of the Free Library of Philadelphia, which serves a forty-thousand-resident, working-class community within a one-mile radius. (Widener had a thirty-five-thousand-item collection.)

One summer's day a teen girl walked into the library, passed my desk, and veered toward the newly designated young adult area. She looked at the shelves; it was apparent she was shelf reading. She then put her hand on her hips, exhaled in exasperation, looked up and down the stack again, and then turned around as if she were looking for someone. I caught her eye, and she walked over to my desk and said:

"Do you have *The Coldest Winter Ever* by Sister Souljah?"

"No, I haven't heard of that one, but we do have her book *No Disrespect*."

"Nah, I saw that. She's got another one now. It's really good. You should get it. For in here."

"Thanks, I will. What's it about?"

"Oooh! It's about this girl who in the 'hood and she a ghetto princess, but then she lose everything, and it's like a rags-to-riches kinda story."

"I'll look into getting it. We have some Bluford books—you wanna try out one of those?"

"Naw, those are corny."

"I'ma see if I can get the new Sister Souljah for you. What's your library card number so I can let you know when it comes in?"

The readers' advisory interaction was completed in usual fashion.

That was the beginning of my decadelong journey into street lit, as we know it today. I do not remember the teen patron's name, but I can attest that the same thing that fascinated me those many years ago when I read a bit of Iceberg Slim was a similar chord to what fascinated this young girl and was calling for her to be a reader of text and story. I could immediately relate to her excitement, her enthusiasm, and her demand.

Thus, I ordered four copies of *The Coldest Winter Ever* and notified the teen patron, whereupon she came back to the library and checked out a copy. The other copies were off the shelf within two days of arrival. As time moved on, teens were coming in asking for Teri Woods's *True to the Game* (1999) and Omar Tyree's *Flyy Girl* ([1996] 1999). I ordered multiple copies of those books also. Again, the books swiftly left the shelves, often returning within days only to be checked out again or eventually lost or stolen. From there, requests came in for *B-More Careful* (2001) by Shannon Holmes and then *Let That Be the Reason* (2002) by Vickie Stringer. I was getting new teen patrons whom I'd never seen before, informing me—no, educating me—on how to make their neighborhood library collection appealing to them.

A phenomenon was brewing as I saw teens I'd never seen before (aside from my core teen patrons) coming off the streets into the library, on their own, during the summer months, asking for books by name and title, and requesting that I order them. The streets had brought street lit into the public library.

During my time at the Widener Branch Library, my young adult collection grew too restrictive and perhaps inappropriate for the street-lit novels because of two developments that occurred simultaneously. First, the genre's publication picked up, with authors like T. N. Baker, Relentless Aaron, Nikki Turner, and Chunichi coming to the fore. Second, the Free Library of Philadelphia acquisitions department was automatically selecting and ordering titles and sending them to branch libraries. With that kind of volume of materials coming in, I created one of the first urban fiction cluster collections in the Free Library (after the incredible librarian Bruce Siebers—who really spearheaded street lit in Philadelphia libraries with no apologies), where I combined the old with the new. Donald Goines and Iceberg Slim, the Black pulp-fiction authors of the 1970s, now had some company on the shelf: authors like Teri Woods, Darren Coleman, Nikki Turner, and K'wan Foye. I created original genre labels in PowerPoint that depicted a city landscape with the words "Urban Fiction." The collection went from its debut on a small rolling book cart to taking up multiple shelves in the fiction stacks.

When I left the Free Library in 2005 to teach library science at Clarion University of Pennsylvania, I subsequently learned that the Widener urban fiction collection was gutted within two weeks of my departure from unbridled circulation, and instead of replacing titles and continuing to develop the cluster, the next librarian consequently dismantled the urban fiction collection. This taught me that perhaps I was one of very few librarians who was advocating for the genre. Given that librarians are taught to be purveyors of the First Amendment and the freedom to read, this experience raised a fascination in me to learn what librarians were thinking and doing about street lit. Seemingly, we were not all regarding this genre with a professional lens reflective of our professional and ethical values as espoused in our profession's Code of Ethics, the "Freedom to Read" statement, the "Libraries: An American Value" statement, and the Library Bill of Rights.

While at Widener, I worked directly with teen readers of the street-lit genre to learn why they read the genre and to facilitate heightening their own understanding of why they read what they read. After I left the Free Library, I came back to Widener as a volunteer (2006–2008) to continue working with the same group of teens. I've also worked with public school teachers and colleague public service librarians to gain a further understanding about educators' resistance to this genre. I've also researched the circulation patterns of major street-lit titles throughout U.S. public libraries, across geographic regions.

By and large, street lit, as we currently understand it, is a prolific genre with a significant readership. Both the genre and its readers will not be denied their voice. It continues to be avidly published, debated, and most important, avidly read. There are now book review websites and blogs focusing on the genre, and scholarly articles are beginning to appear in journals, exploring various aspects of the literature.

As librarians, it is vital that we listen to what this genre has to say. As librarians, it behooves us to care about what our fellow patrons read. What is imperative, as professional librarians, is for us to learn and understand the various characteristics and features of street lit as it demands its presence in the stacks. This requires us, too, to be readers of the genre (i.e., to expand how we read novels, memoirs, poetry, picture books, and graphic novels as street-lit stories), readers of our patrons (i.e., readers' advisory and outreach), and readers of our libraries (i.e., collection development, open and equal access). We must locate ourselves as readers along with the patrons. Thus, as the title of this book denotes, this readers' advisory guide to street literature is addressing librarians to help librarians as readers to read the genre. This book is also an overall readers' guide to street lit, because all of us, patrons and librarians, are readers of genre, the library, and the social interactions that we participate in, within, and beyond library walls. This social literacy is what makes us, as professional librarians and educators, readers and patrons of the very libraries in which we serve. Thus, we are not the only experts in the stacks. The patrons have much to teach us, too.

In this vein, this readers' guide will discuss street lit's appeal to readers (chapter 1), chronicle a history of street literature to situate it along a historical literary continuum (chapter 2), identify the street as a motif for the genre (chapter 3), explore the diversity within the genre itself (chapter 4), and offer up readers' advisory and collection development strategies (chapters 5 and 7). The book also details adult–young adult (A/YA) and teen-friendly street literature and articulates the value of the genre for teen readers (chapter 6). Because a large part of my own theoretical framework for my research focuses on literacy practices as forms of inquiry and reflection, I also discuss how educators, authors, and readers symbiotically participate in the reading of this genre (chapter 8) and the various ways we interact with the genre via library programming and outreach initiatives (chapter 9). The text concludes with an amazing email dialogue between myself, a librarian, and the young adult author Zetta Elliott, with her permission to reproduce the conversation. The dialogue offers a no-holds-barred window into the very conversations that many of us have been hesitant to engage. The epilogue presents the pros and cons of street lit and situates the genre (and its readers) as an ethical and theoretical "given" for librarianship.

Last, at the end of the book you'll find the latest edition of my booklists for public (A/YA) and school (teen-friendly) libraries. The lists reference the titles mentioned throughout the book. I also include a list of salient publishers of street lit, as well as a bibliography of all references cited in this work.

The purpose of this work is to assist the public and/or school librarian, as well as teachers, in gaining an understanding for the genre as professionals and as readers. Street-literature authors and genre readers may find this book useful also. Resources are provided to expand collection and research possibilities.

This is the quest of this humble book. I hope it proves useful to you as a reader, as a lifelong learner, as an educator, as a librarian (which to me is all one and the same). Thanks for listening, and if I could share one thing that I've learned in writing this book, it's this: no book is ever a final draft. I look forward to continued conversations about street literature (feel free to visit my blog, *Street Literature*, at www.streetliterature.com) and continued learning about librarianship—the best profession in the world.

1

"IT'S LIKE A MOVIE IN MY HEAD"
Street Lit and Its Appeal to Readers

Today's renaissance of the street-literature genre appeals to readers for a variety of reasons. One of the main themes of street lit, specifically young adult and adult-oriented novels, is survival: how to survive the streets by circumventing different pitfalls. Readers of the genre, especially teen readers who live in similar settings to those of the stories, say that reading the books teaches them "what not to do, " confirms the fact that "these streets is real," and validates that "this is how it is out here in the hood" (Morris et al. 2006, 22). Readers from outside of inner-city culture say that they learn things about inner-city living they never realized. Many readers are unashamedly, simplistically clear about why street lit appeals to them: because it does; they enjoy reading it.

Street lit is about interpretation and representation. It is a genre that provides an interpretive lens through which readers witness the daily survival struggles and dramas of city residents living certain lifestyles. These lifestyles are varied, from the pimp and prostitute to the working single mom and stories about the detective and the news anchor. This genre is called many things and is classified haphazardly at times. However, to appropriately situate street lit, with all its diversity in stories, characters, and settings, we must look at the genre from the widened lens of urbanity.

URBAN, CITY, 'HOOD: LOCATING STREET LIT

There's been some debate about what to call this genre. Is it urban fiction? What does it mean to be urban fiction as compared to, say, rural fiction? Is it hip-hop lit? Ghetto lit? What do we call this thing commonly called street lit?

"Urban fiction" denotes stories set in urban settings. When we say "urban," we are talking about major cities, like New York, Philadelphia, Baltimore, Chicago, Los Angeles, and New Orleans, to name a few. We are talking about major cities where the population density is dense. There are urban cities all over the world—Paris, Rome, London, and the most urban city on the planet, Tokyo. So when we say "urban fiction" we're talking about a huge range of characters and experiences that span cultural, social, political, geographical, and economic boundaries. Thus, urban fiction can encompass genres such as chick lit, lad lit, urban fantasy, speculative fiction, urban erotica (e.g., Zane), and street lit, because many stories in these genres are situated in established urban settings.

Urban areas often feature enclaves of neighborhoods that ascribe to particular cultural representations. For example, many urban areas have a Chinatown or a Little Italy to denote enclaves where specific cultural groups live and thrive. In kind, neighborhoods can be named with specific designations to denote socioeconomic status, such as saying that an enclave where poverty is prevalent is "the ghetto." Without going into the historicity of the origin and use of the word *ghetto*, we all understand that in common, current use, the term denotes a low-income, albeit impoverished, city neighborhood. With the advent of hip-hop culture, the term *the 'hood* has appropriated *the ghetto*. Additionally, the term *the 'hood* can denote where you live, regardless of your socioeconomic status.

WHAT MAKES STREET LIT, STREET LIT

In thinking about how street literature can be defined, or if it is even definable, one thing is consistent and clear: street literature is location and setting specific. It is a genre in which the stories, be they fiction or nonfiction, are consistently set in urban, inner-city enclaves. Settings may shift as characters travel in the stories, but basically, what makes a street-fiction story a street-fiction story is that it is set in inner-city streets.

Thus, the overall qualifying characteristic of street lit is that it is location specific. Street lit of yesteryear and today, by and large, depicts tales about the daily lives of people living in lower-income city neighborhoods. This characteristic spans historical timelines, as well as various cultural identifications, linguistic associations, and formats. For example, this means that a street-lit story can be from the 1800s (historical timeline) about an Irish immigrant family living in the ghetto (cultural identifications), speaking an Americanized Irish dialect (linguistic associations), and rendered as a novella (format). Indeed, Stephen Crane's *Maggie: A Girl of the Streets*, published in 1893, is just such a tome. Street literature was also published as early as the sixteenth century and into the mid-nineteenth century in the form of broadsides—large, poster-sized, print publications that told the news stories, songs, writings, and announcements of the neighborhood (Shepard 1973). Truth be told, broadsides and street pamphlets were precursors to the newspaper industry as we know it today. The way citizens communicate and navigate daily news has always come from the streets (Shepard 1973).

CHARACTERISTICS OF STREET LIT

Aside from being stories set in and depicting the livelihood of lower-income city neighborhoods, the prevailing characteristics of street lit are the following:

- fast-paced stories, often with flashback sequences
- vivid depictions of the inner-city environment, including lack of societal resources, substandard housing, and poverty
- the street as an interactive stage (things happen on the street or because of the street)
- female and male identity formation (via intense relationships, often romantic in nature), with protagonists often being young adults (common age range is nineteen to twenty-five)
- navigation of interpersonal relationships, including surviving abuse, betrayal in friendships, fantastical revenge plots
- commodification of lifestyles (name-brand this, bling-bling that)
- surviving street life and overcoming street lifestyle—the challenge of moving up and away from the streets

These characteristics are not exclusive. There are other characteristics that may come and go within street lit; therefore, street-lit elements cross and blend with other literary genres, such as romance (e.g., Tracy Brown's *Black*, 2003), mystery (e.g., Solomon Jones's *The Bridge*, 2003), speculative (e.g., Zetta Elliott's *A Wish after Midnight*, 2010), and even science fiction (e.g., Octavia Butler's *Mind of My Mind*, 1977). Some scholars and educators might prefer to point to more gritty themes common in street lit, such as the illegal drug trade and drug use, domestic violence, and possibly stereotypical gender representations of characters as definitive characteristics of the genre. However, these themes are not necessarily uniquely characteristic of street lit, as these themes occur in genres throughout Western literary tradition (e.g., romance novels, as researched in Janice Radway's 1991 *Reading the Romance*; the role of women authors in horror novels as discussed in a *New York Times* article from October 24, 2008, "Shelley's Daughters"). Such marginalizing themes are not necessarily indicative of, or unique to, street lit. But what is unique and peculiar to street lit is what I have determined as the overall qualifying characteristic of street lit—stories that depict realistic, naturalistic tales about the daily lives of people living in lower-income city neighborhoods. This opens our perception of street lit to include literature and formats that span life stages and cultural experiences. This overall qualifying characteristic of street lit also connects contemporary street literature with the literary tradition of naturalism, in which "characters can be studied through their relationships to their surroundings" (Campbell 2010, para. 1) and in which there exists tension between interpretation of experience and "aesthetic recreation of experience" (Pizer, quoted in Campbell 2010, para. 4).

With the given characteristics in mind, we can see how readers, especially in various city locations are attracted to this genre. This genre tells their stories as interpretations and re-creations of scenes and activities that realistically occur in daily life. Readers enjoy reading about what they know and live. It makes readers feel competent in their reading because they are reading stories that they can relate to and understand. It makes readers feel competent in their own interpretation of their lived life. This kind of reader response is true for the preschooler, the school-age child, the teen, the adult, and the senior; it is true for the teacher, the librarian, the author, and the reader.

"IT'S LIKE A MOVIE IN MY HEAD"

Readers of young adult and adult street-lit novels have been recorded as saying, "That's not me in the story, but I know that girl. I see her walking down the street" (author's field notes, 2007). Others have said, "It's like a movie in my head" (D. Marcou, personal communication, 2009). Both statements attest to the ability of the reader to see their own reality reflected in street-lit stories but are also clear that it's not real life; it is indeed like a movie in one's head, a fiction. This idea of a movie in the head also speaks to the imagination being ignited during the reading of a street-lit story. This attests to the success of the genre in terms of igniting the reading habit in people who perhaps were not readers before.

Young adult and some adult readers have also shared that before street lit, they didn't have anything to read that appealed to them, that was authentic or "real." Teen readers, in particular, have stated with a huge sense of accomplishment that it wasn't until they read *True to the Game* or *The Coldest Winter Ever* that they were able to complete a novel from cover to cover. Thus, street lit holds the power to transform reluctant readers into lifelong readers. One public librarian at the Philadelphia Librarian Book Club in November 2009 reflected on the appeal of street lit: "We create the street. We create the pain, the poverty, the violence. The street is a blank canvas and we humans are the artists who have painted the picture. It is us. The street is us." Street lit appeals to readers because it offers an opportunity to investigate, validate, and/or make sense of the details of city life.

STREET LIT'S STRUCTURAL ELEMENTS

A street-literature novel's structure is unique for the following elements: language, format, appealing book covers, and double-entendre titles. When it comes to the style of writing, street lit has long been derided for not being well edited or well written. This was true for the earlier days of the renaissance, and it may still hold true for some entrepreneurial works that lack the benefit of an editor or editorial staff. However, by and large, with major publishing houses like Simon and Schuster and St. Martin's Press embracing street-lit authors and creating imprint presses to feature the genre (e.g., Dafina's Kensington Books), the editorial integrity of the genre has vastly improved. Also, as independent street-lit publishers, such as Triple Crown Publications, have gained experience with editing and publishing texts, their quality of product has improved as well. In addition, readers, as they become experts of the genre, straightforwardly complain and demand that authors produce clean, tight, well-developed works. You can read virtually any street-lit customer review on Amazon .com, for example, and realize that for readers a sloppily produced book greatly diminishes the credibility and appeal of the author. Readers may forgive the authors for their debut novel or for a dud in the middle of a series, but if subsequent publications are sloppily rendered, readers may express frustration and exhibit keenly what their expectations are for a well-drafted street-lit novel. For example, one reader's comment from May 2003 on Amazon.com for Wahida Clark's debut novel, *Thugs and the Women Who Love Them* (2004), read: "This book was so bad I couldn't even finnish [*sic*] reading it. In the first story the 'pimp' character was sooooo unbelievable. It struck me more as a first draft, not a completely edited book."

Years later, Wahida Clark is now a major author and publisher in the street-lit genre, having spearheaded her own subgenre, known as thug-love fiction, of which she is colloquially referred to as the Queen of Thug-Love Fiction. However, even after penning eight titles, with one appearing on the New York Times Best-Seller List at one point, readers can be ruthlessly critical and demanding. Even while street-lit readers demand that stories "keep it real," they also passionately demand that authors "get it right." Case in point, sixteen readers gave Clark's seventh published title, *Thug Lovin'* (2009), a one-star (out of five stars) review. Here is what one of those customer reviewers said on Amazon.com in August 2009:

> I have no idea what book all these people who said this book deserved 3, 4, or 5 stars because on its best day it's not even a 2. I waited for this book even preordered it as soon as I could. To say that I hated this book is an understatement, I feel like I was conned. . . . While reading, I kept wondering what the author's mind set was when she wrote this book, her thoughts were all over the place, and so were the characters. Events seemed out of place almost like they belonged to another story all together, and the ending made me want to scream. I will not even talk about how Trae turned into a complete asshole or how Tasha and Kyra went from being classy well educated women to, women who allowed there [*sic*] once lovin husbands to make them hoes, all in the name of revenge. The ending of the book should have been the middle, and the story should have continued from there. I see now why this book was pushed back from (publication) April 09 to August 09. If the next book in this series is as bad as this one Wahida should just hang up her crown.

Social media contributions, such as online customer book reviews, provide valuable feedback and insight into the ongoing appeal and standards within street lit and reader responses. This conveys how valuable reader response is with determining the direction of the genre. As of this writing, *Thug Lovin'* has received 231 customer reviews on Amazon.com, with only 18 conferring a one-star review. However, the feedback from such low-graded reviews is an important critique that contributes to the author's relationship with his or her reader fan base, thus informing authors and publishers of what appeals to readers of the genre. Such reviews confirm the reality that, yes, readers demand quality literature, even from the pantheon of street-lit authors.

Language

Decidedly, contemporary street lit is an African American–focused genre, meaning that most of the mainstream novels today feature African American protagonists and antagonists, as well as elements of African American Vernacular English (AAVE), hip-hop slang, and American regional dialects. Though framed primarily around Standard American English (SAE), linguistically street lit is diverse. In addition to AAVE, elements of Jamaican patois, Haitian Creole, Caribbean Spanish, and West African languages underlie the SAE linguistic foundation, depending on the story.

Street lit is known for its unapologetic use of AAVE, regional dialect, and slang. This does not mean that the books are badly written. It means that the genre is written with a target audience in mind who is literate in this language and can read it. In terms of its literariness, the writings of authors such as Sister Souljah, Shannon Holmes, Tracy Brown, and K'wan Foye come to mind as possessing mainstream literary quality. That is not to say that other authors in the genre do not write literarily. I posit that such a determination ultimately lies in the mind of the reader.

Format

Street lit can also be presented with a blended format. In addition to the usual prose in which novels typically occur, there are also street-lit epistolaries (e.g., Kalisha Buckhanon's *Upstate*, 2005), stories with poetry interspersed throughout the story (see *True to the Game* by Teri Woods, 1999, and *Black* by Tracy Brown, 2003), and illustrated stories (see *Midnight: A Gangster Love Story* by Sister Souljah, 2008).

Because the prevailing qualifying characteristic of street lit is location specific, set in low-income city neighborhoods (other synonyms are the inner city, the ghetto, and the 'hood), we can find street-lit stories in various formats, such as poetry, picture books, and graphic novels.

There are picture books that depict inner-city living, such as Ezra Jack Keats's 1962 classic *The Snowy Day*, in which we are introduced to the first depiction of an African American protagonist in picture books, the illustrious Peter. The question can be asked, Is this street fiction? *The Snowy Day* is a story about Peter, about five years old, walking the streets of Harlem (alone) on a snowy day, where he makes snow angels and even realizes he's too young to participate in snowball fights. Is this street fiction? From a child's point of view, would this be a story of a successful day surviving on the streets? What about Keats's later story, *Goggles!* (1969), when Peter is a bit older. In this picture book, Peter and his friend Archie have a run-in with a street gang.

Many, many picture books depict street survival—too countless to list here. But some salient titles include *We Are All in the Dumps with Jack and Guy* by Maurice Sendak (1993), *Tar Beach* by Faith Ringgold (1996), *Brothers of the Knight* by Debbie Allen and Kadir Nelson (2001), *Neighborhood Mother Goose* by Nina Crews (2003), and *My Feet Are Laughing* by Lissette Norman and Frank Morrison (2006).

There are also graphic novels that depict inner-city living, as well as many established young adult fiction authors who tell stories of the streets, such as Walter Dean Myers (notably his recently published poetry book *Street Love*, 2006, and the novel *Dopesick*, 2009); Sharon Flake (*Bang!*, 2005, and *Who Am I without Him?* (2004), a short-story compilation that includes a heart-wrenching letter from a father in prison to his daughter); Kalisha Buckhanon (*Upstate*, 2005, an epistolary that spans a decade); and Janet McDonald, whose many titles for tweeners (school-age readers typically in grades 5–8) include *Twists and Turns* (2003), *Brother Hood* (2004), and *Chill Wind* (2006). Notably, McDonald's autobiography (for young adult audiences), *Project Girl* (2000), was a graphic detailing of her struggles from transitioning from being a ghetto girl in Brooklyn to a scholarship college girl at Vassar College, where she acquired a heroin addiction.

Book Covers

The covers of street-lit novels are often full-colored depictions of young adults in urban settings, dressed in contemporary street wear. The covers may sometimes be sexually suggestive, with certain poses enacted that suggest romance between male and female characters. The covers have been criticized over the years for objectifying female bodily representation and glorifying male attitudes of machismo. Critics complain that with these representations, the book covers underscore stereotypical assumptions about inner-city young adults and adults as oversexualized.

It is apparent that some authors or publishers have moved away from this type of imagery on the book covers. For example, Sister Souljah's book covers are invariably colorful and attractive to a reader's eye, but the imagery conveys a sense of mystery about the protagonist: Winter's eyes are gazing sternly through a haze of blue and fuchsia on the cover of *The Coldest Winter Ever*, and on Souljah's second novel, *Midnight: A Gangster Love Story* (2008), the main character, Midnight, is depicted as a beautiful, black-skinned teen boy looking askance with a gaze to the future—again amid a haze of the mysterious purplish hue. Teri Woods opts for bold, primary colors for her book covers, with the book titles boldly displayed to demand attention. Her book covers rarely, if ever, feature people or faces.

Triple Crown Publications, by far the largest independent street-lit publishing house, boasting more than forty authors, provides picturesque book covers that boldly show photogenic African American characters amid urban backdrops standing in groups to denote a multiprotagonist story, or perhaps softer, romantic poses of characters to denote a romantic story. Patrons are known to come into the library and ask for Triple Crown novels by brand name as opposed to title and author. Most Triple Crown novels are branded on the book cover with the name Triple Crown Publications. The colorful, photographic look of the covers appeals to readers of street lit because they can relate to the urban depictions of the clothing, jewelry, and backdrops displayed. If readers do not remember the author or title of a book, they will often be able to convey what book they are referring to through a description of the book cover.

Titles

Book titles for street lit are often double entendres of street slang expressions. For example, Shannon Holmes's *B-More Careful* means literally "be more careful" but also denotes the locally recognized colloquial reference for the city of Baltimore as "B-More." Thus, the title also means "Baltimore careful" to convey the setting of the story and the inherent dangers of the Baltimore streets that the story depicts. Both meanings can be convoluted into an interwoven understanding to be careful on the streets of Baltimore. This kind of titling is an ingenious use of language to convey a lot of meaning with few words. Readers invariably know and understand the loaded meanings embedded within the titles.

Another example comes from the foremost classic of the contemporary street-lit renaissance: *The Coldest Winter Ever*. We can take the title to mean a cold time, a span of all that the coldest winter indicates: isolation, lack (of warmth, of ease of survival, of sun), lack of happiness and good times, survival by any means necessary. When we learn that the protagonist's name is also Winter, the title takes on another meaning to project Winter's character as icy, mean, and raw, in addition to all the characteristics of a literal coldest winter. Colloquially, in the 'hood, to be "cold" is to be cutthroat, ruthless, and heartless. Indeed, Winter Santiaga exhibits all those qualities in the story.

The double entendre is common in street-lit titles. We could also further examine *Push* (1996) by Sapphire, *Grimey* (2004) by KaShamba Williams, Quentin Carter's *Hoodwinked* (2005), and Keisha Ervin's *Hold U Down* (2006) as further examples of this formulaic double-entendre titling of street-lit novels, which has proved a very effective marketing tool to appeal to readers.

2

FROM *MOLL FLANDERS* TO *THE COLDEST WINTER EVER*
A Historical Timeline of Street Lit

The street-lit form of American urban fiction is not a new genre. During the mid-1960s and 1970s, narratives such as Claude Brown's *Manchild of the Promised Land* (1965), Malcolm X's autobiography (1965), and Donald Goines's two semiautobiographical series, *Dopefiend* (1971) and *Whoreson* (1972), graphically and realistically depicted the harsh, gritty lifestyles of inner-city African Americans. Just as today, in yesteryear food was hard to come by, some people preyed on the innocence of children, and violence was always a force to be reconciled. There continues to be high circulation of these older street-lit titles, including titles by Iceberg Slim, who was another prolific street-lit author during the 1970s, with titles such as *Pimp: The Story of My Life*, 1969, and *Mama Black Widow: A Story of the South's Black Underworld*, 1969. The continuous need for public libraries to provide multiple copies of Malcolm X's autobiography as well as titles like *Monster: The Autobiography of a L.A. Gang Member* by Sanyika Shakur (2004), Nathan McCall's *Makes Me Wanna Holler* (1995), and *Down These Mean Streets* by Piri Thomas (1967) illustrates how nonfiction street literature is also a significant aspect of the street-lit genre.

When we consider authors like Charles Dickens, Stephen Crane, and Upton Sinclair, we can understand that literary fictions have been telling uncompromising stories of marginalized Americans for centuries. In the late nineteenth century, the genre mainly focused on the ghetto lives of European immigrants in New York's inner-city slums. One example is Stephen Crane's debut novel, *Maggie: A Girl of the Streets* (1893).

The story is about the brutal, impoverished daily lives of Irish residents in a New York City slum. Just like in today's street novels, the men in *Maggie* were characterized as frustrated, demoralized, and violent, whereas the women were depicted as melodramatic, hard-hearted, confused, and depressed. In Crane's *Maggie*, everyone is addicted to something, be it alcohol, power, or sex, and the tale (as typical in today's street lit) does not have a happy ending. Just like Teri Woods in 1999, Stephen Crane in 1893 struggled to find a publisher for his debut novel; publishers found the novella too graphic and that it "reeked of sexual realism." Indeed, publishers rebuked:

> *Maggie: A Girl of the Streets* is a shockingly explicit portrait of the brutal conditions that existed in the poverty-stricken slums of New York. Originally refused by all publishers that it was submitted to because of its brutal and sexual realism, *Maggie: A Girl of the Streets* was first published by Stephen Crane at his own expense. (Back cover, *Digireads.com* classic edition, original publication, 1893)

Crane ultimately self-published the novel under a pseudonym. It was only after the publishing success of his classic *The Red Badge of Courage* (1895) that Crane was able to publish a second edition of *Maggie* using his real name (Stallman 1955). Today *Maggie* is considered a literary classic and a solid text in the American literary canon. Other so-called slum novels of the period include Frank Norris's *McTeague* (1899) and Abraham Cahan's *Yekl: A Tale of the New York Ghetto* (1896) (Randal 1993). Together with Crane's *Maggie*, these works helped spark a literary movement known as naturalism (Campbell 2010).

Taking all of these various locations for street stories into account, it is clear that the contemporary renaissance of street lit (which started in 1999)—published nowadays under the auspices of Triple Crown Publications, Simon and Schuster imprints, St. Martin's Griffin, RP Publications, and a host of other publishing outlets—does not sit alone and isolated on library and bookstore shelves. When we look at contemporary street-lit novels such as *The Coldest Winter Ever* (1999), *Dirty Game* (2007), and *Thugs for Life* (2009), we can understand that they exist along a historical continuum of literature that tells similar stories in different time periods (as well as an age continuum—such as picture books for little children and young adult novels for teens). But they all tell stories about the street.

"THE STREETS" SUPPORT STREET LIT

When considering competing definitions for street literature, it is a matter not just of who is publishing street literature but also of who is writing street lit today. It is not unheard of for the publisher and the author to be one and the same. There are many titles that are sold literally just on the streets—on the tables of street vendors across American cities. This entrepreneurial pattern is also historical in nature. Just as Teri Woods sold her first novel, *True to the Game* (1999), and Vickie Stringer sold her debut work, *Let That Be the Reason* (2002), from the trunks of their cars, we are reminded of Stephen Crane's struggle during the 1890s when he, too, had to self-publish *Maggie.* Authors sell their works on the streets for one major reason: major publishers reject their work. And publishers have always rejected street lit for the same reasons, be it the 1890s or the 1990s—because the work is too raw, gritty, graphic, violent, and sexual.

Harlem Renaissance works such as Ann Petry's *The Street* (1946) and Richard Wright's *Native Son* (1940) can also be perceived as street lit. In Petry's novel, the protagonist, Lutie Johnson, is always fighting against the power of the street:

> Suppose she got used to it, took it for granted, became resigned to it and all the things it represented. The thought set her to murmuring aloud, "I mustn't get used to it. Not ever. I've got to keep on fighting to get away from here." . . . Because this street and the other streets just like it would, if he [her son] stayed in them long enough, do something terrible to him. Sooner or later they would do something equally as terrible to her. And as she sat there in the dark, she began to think about the things she had seen on such streets as this one she lived in. (194)

Richard Wright saw the street as a creator of consciousness and recognized that during his lifetime, African Americans "possessed no fictional works dealing with such problems, and had no background in such sharp and critical testing of experience, no novels that went with a deep and fearless will down to the dark roots of life" (Wright 1940, xvi). In his introduction to *Native Son*, in an essay titled "How Bigger Was Born," Wright shares that he learned how to apply behavioral realities of the streets to the creation of his protagonist, Bigger Thomas, by reading texts about other streets beyond U.S. shores, specifically in London and Russia. Indeed, he said: "Actions and feelings of men ten thousand miles from home helped me to understand the moods and impulses of those walking the streets of Chicago and Dixie" (xvii). Richard Wright connected the frustrations of poverty, segregation, hegemony, and injustice as a human condition that was commonly acted out in ghettos across the globe.

During the civil rights era, works that depicted inner-city living and survival included Claude Brown's (1937–2002) fictionalized autobiography, the now-classic *Manchild of the Promised Land* (1965) and the perennial

Autobiography of Malcolm X (1965) by Alex Haley and Malcolm X (1925–1965). In both texts, the authors' lives are chronicled to reveal harsh realities and truths about growing up in the inner city and, more important, the challenges in successfully navigating coming of age into adulthood in low-income city environments. Case in point, Malcolm X's autobiography continues to be on high school reading lists in schools across the country. For example, Carver High School in Aldine, Texas, had the title on its 2009 summer reading list, and Attleboro High School in Massachusetts had the title, along with Dickens's *Oliver Twist* (a story about a street urchin and the abuses he experiences in nineteenth-century London) on its summer reading list for the 2010–2011 academic year. As previously noted, forty-five years after its initial publication, the Malcolm X autobiography continues to be a regularly circulated book in public libraries. *Manchild of the Promised Land* can still be found on many public and school library shelves as well, as it, too, is often required reading for high schools (Worth 2002).

In an obituary for Claude Brown, Worth cites the book critic Irving Howe's underscoring of the importance of Brown's seminal work: "What many of us talk about in abstractions . . . is here given the quivery reality of a boy's life, his struggle, his efforts at understanding. This book contributes to our sense of what America is today" (quoted in Worth 2002, para. 4). If we go back a bit further along the literary timeline, we can see that street literature (as survival stories about the streets) was written about the American inner-city experiences of Irish (Stephen Crane's *Maggie: A Girl of the Streets*, 1893), Jewish (Abraham Cahan's *Yekl: A Tale of the New York Ghetto*, 1896), and Italian (Mario Puzo's *The Fortunate Pilgrim*, 1965 but set in the 1920s) immigrant families.

We could also delve into British canonical literature to identify stories about survival in the streets with such titles as Daniel Defoe's *Moll Flanders* (1722), Charles Dickens's *Oliver Twist* (1838), and Israel Zangwill's *Children of the Ghetto* (1892).

STREET LIT'S HISTORICAL CONTINUUM

It is apparent that the voices of those who live challenging lives in low-income city enclaves use literature as a vehicle to be heard. We are reminded of street literature in the format of broadsides, which are poster-sized newsprints with text on both sides of the paper, chronicling local neighborhood news (Shepard 1973). Street literature has a five-hundred-year publication history in the format of broadsides and chapbooks, where ballads, poems, short stories, anthologies, and community information (ancestral "tweets") were published regularly for the masses. During Victorian times, while the aristocracy was reading Dickens's *Oliver Twist* (1838) and *A Tale of Two Cities* (1859) with privileged fascination, the people who those stories were about were reading street literature in the form of broadsides and chapbooks that sustained their authentic street culture (Shepard 1973).

The story of a teen girl who is prostituted in the streets of London during the early eighteenth century (*Moll Flanders*); an orphan boy who witnesses horrible violence at the hand of a greedy adult gang leader of vagrant kids in the early nineteenth century (*Oliver Twist*); the harsh, violent interactions of an Irish family struggling to adjust to late-nineteenth-century American life (*Maggie: A Girl of the Streets*); the heartbreaking losses overcome by an early-twentieth-century Italian immigrant family able to move away from the tenements of New York City (*The Fortunate Pilgrim*); the struggles of a Harlem Renaissance single mom who is lost in the wind while trying to make a life for herself and son in Harlem (*The Street*); the deep fear and intense rage of a disenfranchised African American young adult male living in poverty in the tale of *Native Son*—street lit tells the stories of everyday people living intense realities as they struggle to realize the American dream.

Such street survival stories continued to be published during the civil rights era of the mid-twentieth century with works from Claude Browne, Chester Himes, and Malcolm X. The 1970s brought the rise of ghetto pulp-fiction novels that detailed the seedy, underworld side of inner-city living. In the prolific works of Donald Goines and Iceberg Slim, we learn about the daily experiences of the dope fiend and the pimp as everyday people who find themselves ensconced in this underworld environment because of lack of access to experiences beyond that environment. Goines and Slim rendered raw, gritty, realistic portraits of street life, often painting intense characterizations of drug addicts, dope dealers, and their struggles to navigate or to even overcome the lure and call of the streets. Goines's and Slim's works coincided with the 1970s Blaxploitation film era, in which movies were often telling similar stories about inner-city living, with films such as *Shaft* (1971), *Super Fly* (1972), *Cleopatra Jones* (1973), and *Trick Baby* (1973, an adaptation of Slim's novel of the same name).

Similarly, the 1990s brought about the high point of hip-hop as a musical and cultural force. Coinciding with the emerging hip-hop movement were films about the urban Black experience by directors such as Spike Lee, John Singleton, and the Hughes brothers. Films such as Lee's *Do the Right*

Thing (1989), Singleton's *Boyz n the Hood* (1991), and the Hughes brothers' *Menace II Society* (1993) told the tales of tensions and struggles that were still prevalent on the streets of low-income, minority city neighborhoods. The tales are similar to the immigrant ghetto tales of the early twentieth century—tales of struggles with the city environment, with assimilating into mainstream American culture, and with coping with the daily living frustrations of various abuses (substance, physical, street violence).

During the twentieth century, street lit was primarily a European immigrant story, and during the early twenty-first century, it is primarily an African American and Latino story, with novels about diverse African American and Latino characters, such as Ceazia (pronounced "Cee-Asia") Devereaux, a biracial girl from an upper-middle-class background in Chunichi's Gangster Girl series (2004–2009). The ruthless gangster Dutch in Teri Woods's Dutch trilogy (2004–2011) fights an African drug lord to claim his empire, and alongside him is his right-hand lieutenant, the hard-knocks Latina Angel. In Black Artemis's *Explicit Content* (2004), Latina Leila Aponte and African American Cassie Rivers are best friends whose friendship is sorely tested as they climb their ladder to hip-hop stardom. The historicity of street literature isn't chronicling cultural norms or stereotypes about certain ethnic groups inasmuch as chronicling the challenging socioeconomic realities of diverse peoples, *whomever they may be,* who are living in low-income city communities at various periods in time.

Thus, the current renaissance of the street-literature genre is documenting the historicity of inner-city living in the late twentieth and early twenty-first centuries, when the residents happen to be diasporic African American, Latino, and even Asian and white people (see Souljah's *Midnight: A Gangster Love Story*). Such diverse experiences have been documented musically in hip-hop and in its various iterations, cinematically in various films from the 1990s and early 2000s, and literarily since the mid- to late 1990s in street lit.

FICTION AND NONFICTION: STREET LIT ON BOTH SIDES OF THE AISLE

It is interesting that street literature comes from so many voices, spaces, places, ideas, and positions, yet the stories are all about one common theme—surviving the streets. Even nonfiction scholarly ethnographic works have been published about surviving street life and inner-city living, such as works by Elijah Anderson (1999, 2009), Katherine S. Newman (1999, 2003), Alex Kotlowitz (1992), David K. Shipler (2005), Geoffrey Canada (1995), William Julius Wilson (2009), and Sudhir Venkatesh (2006, 2008).

It should also be noted that many current-day fictional works are written by women (Souljah, Woods, Stringer, Wahida Clark, Nikki Turner, and many more), but it seems that the bulk of the nonfiction socioanthropological works are written by men. It is evident that there are gender-based underpinnings at work here (Marshall, Staples, and Gibson 2009), but we must also acknowledge the time-honored literary preferences of women for reading fiction and of men for reading nonfiction. Thus, it is not a far stretch that the majority of street-lit authors are women, and the majority of nonfiction street literature authors are men. If you put the two sides of the aisle together, you have a literature collection that has always existed on personal, public, and school library shelves. What was before considered trash or risqué is now considered canonical.

It should also be noted that there are poetry works that speak to the street and urban experience, with contributions such as Tupac Shakur's *The Rose That Grew from Concrete* (1999), a hugely popular book in public libraries for many years after its publication. Another example of an important poetry work that gives voice to inner-city living is Jill Scott's *The Moments, the Minutes, the Hours: The Poetry of Jill Scott* (2005). Other standard poetry works from the young adult collection that detail city realities of youths include Helen Frost's *Keesha's House* (2007), Walter Dean Myers's *Street Love* (2006), and Lori Marie Carlson's *Red Hot Salsa: Bilingual Poems on Being Young and Latino in the United States* (2005), to name a few.

History tells us that just as the nineteenth- and early-twentieth-century slum novels now hold their respectable place on library shelves as renderings of historical fiction, such will be the case for the current iterations of street literature as well. Although we may not expect such titles like *Hood Rat* (2006) by K'wan to be considered canonical based on title alone, such a work like *Hoodlum: A Novel* (2005), also penned by K'wan, holds the possibility for standing the test of time and sitting alongside titles such as *Native Son* (Wright 1940) or *All Shot Up* (Himes 1960) or *Always Outnumbered, Always Outgunned* (Mosley 1997). Sister Souljah has definitely made an impact on the literary world with *The Coldest Winter Ever*, which is being read and studied in college classrooms across the country (including in courses I teach).

History also tells us that just as certain titles rose to the top of the pile to hold their place on bookshelves for decades (surely we understand that Crane's *Maggie* and Paul Laurence Dunbar's 1902 *The Sport of the Gods* weren't the only books of their kind published at the time), the same will happen for the street literature of today. It is clear that readers have the final say on what stays on the shelf and what does not. As librarians and educators, it is up to us to respect and honor readers' reading choices.

3

THE STREETS ARE CALLIN'
The Streets as a Literary Motif

"The street" can be perceived as a character in and of itself. The street summons, it judges, it motivates, it influences. Characters make decisions based on what is happening or not happening in the street. Characters often take heed to "the word on the street." This gives the streets a characterization that has voice; thus, it possesses power to inform, misinform, to shout, and to silence characters. This fictional characterization of the streets is inspired by real-life conceptions of what the streets are and what the streets can do to people and communities. Hip-hop as a culture clearly demonstrates the streets as a powerful symbolism for living life. If I were to imagine a mathematical representation of the streets as a motif in hip-hop music, film, drama, and literature, it would be a very simple equation: street = life. In our context for literature, we can see how street lit is indeed really life lit.

Through many discussions about street lit during the past decade or so that it has been thriving in the publishing industry, various elements of the genre have been problematized and critiqued in terms of the social, cultural, literary, and possibly moral messages that the genre voices. Academic scholars, frontline educators, and some African American authors have been engaged in a mild debate over the years, critiquing the characterizations of women and men in street lit, the dramatic plotlines, graphic sex scenes, and violent action scenes (Chiles 2006; McMillan 2007; McFadden 2010; Pernice 2010).

Even though "the streets" are referred to and deferred to as an overall theme, character, or "silent antagonist" (as I call the streets on my blog) of the street-lit genre, there has been no real exploration of the symbolism of the streets or unpacking of the nuanced meaning(s) of the streets or any thoughtful treatment of the streets as a motif for storytelling in the street-lit genre.

On my blog, *Street Literature*, I write about the street as a silent antagonist:

> The street, in and of itself, can be considered a motif for street literature texts because the street itself is often characterized as an awakened, ominous presence that speaks as an expression of nature's cycles of seasons, coagulated thoughts, words, and deeds. The street is a silent antagonist. It never speaks in language or in voice. It speaks through the gaps in silence—the exhale, the gasp before the breath—the street speaks. It demands response to the blood it sheds, as if a sacrificial altar upon which souls are summoned to purgatory. The street positions itself as a necessary rite of passage in order to reach that American dream (whatever that may be). The street is an unnatural hell where through elevation of the mind (education) emancipation is not only possible, but inevitable. ("Precious—The Response" 2009)

Although this commentary might sound a bit esoteric, the thrust of the posting is that the streets function as a stage on which powerful and meaningful acts of living are actualized and negotiated.

When we say "the streets," we are talking about the actual streets that connect and intersect city neighborhoods. The streets denote territorial boundaries that define a group of residents who live in a certain area. In this vein, "the streets" is synonymous with "the 'hood." The streets can also be perceived as having their own identity or force that informs and influences actions and behaviors of those who frequent, interact, and conduct business (i.e., hustle) on the streets. That is why when you read a street-lit novel, the street in and of itself is oftentimes characterized as if it were a living, breathing entity that interacts with characters, thereby influencing and perhaps determining their decisions, activities, and fates.

As a motif, the streets symbolize possibility and the enactment of choice; it is an ominous, mysterious, four-sided intersection with no directional signs. Its power is a historical pileup of varied peoples walking, talking, sitting, lingering, playing, and observing life as it unfolds on the stage of the streets. Inner-city residents recognize instinctively that the streets hold a wisdom, if you will, a memory of transactions and interactions that metaphysically informs those who live there. For example, the characters of Miz Cleo and Miz Osecola in Meesha Mink and De'nesha Diamond's Bentley Manor Tales series (2008–2009) are depictions of inner-city residents who have survived the streets; recognize and respect its power; and sit and observe younger generations test, submit, negotiate, and reconcile with the streets.

When we think of the scene of Lutie Johnson surveying 116th Street in Harlem while looking for a place to live for her and her son in Ann Petry's *The Street* or Dutch's swagger as he walks commanding deference in his 'hood in Teri Woods's *Dutch*, or Jada's frustration and confusion as she wanders the streets when she leaves her mother's home to escape abuse in Tracy Brown's *White Lines: A Novel* (2007), we can see how the street is a presence but also an anthropomorphic embodiment, almost a narrator of its own scenery.

Street lit often paints the streets as this cold, fast-paced chaotic thruway where characters fearfully and quickly move from one place to another, dodging looming dangers. In this vein, fictionalized streets realistically parallel realities lived in real life. Case in point, fifteen-year-old Tony (personal names throughout are pseudonyms) admitted to his book club once that he's scared when he walks the streets in the mornings to school because he "don' know what dudes be doin' on the corners or walkin' pass me" (teen book club meeting, Philadelphia, August 2007). Another book clubber, thirteen-year-old Debbie, echoed Tony's fears, adding that she, too, is afraid when walking in the 'hood. Meanwhile, seventeen-year-old Cheron said it best: "You go through challenges before you even leave the house. Lotta times there's drama in the home that you gotta deal wit' before you even hit the streets."

One aspect of "the streets" as a motif is its power to converge the public (outside home) with the private (inside home). The streets' chaos oftentimes inserts itself into unfolding dramas inside the home. The dramas in street-literature stories (fiction and nonfiction) chronicle how behavior and interactions from the streets continue to play out inside the home. One example of the streets moving into the home is vividly depicted by Donald Goines in his novel *Dopefiend*. In this story, the protagonist Terry presents herself as a middle-class working girl while in the streets, but once inside Porky's drug house, where she begins to ingest street drugs, her inside persona seeps outside, and ultimately, as a drug addict, her private and public personas become one.

When we look at street lit along a historical continuum, we see how characters' movement through the streets is often deterministic. For example, protagonists like Moll Flanders, Oliver Twist, and Winter Santiaga experience their rise and fall in the streets.

Moll Flanders and Oliver Twist are street urchins, parentless people who come of age in the streets. For them, the fall is their tough childhoods, and their rise is their coming of age. For Winter, her rise, via her father's command of the streets because of his drug empire, confers status and prestige for her at a young age. Winter's fall occurs during her coming of age, on the streets, when Bullet sets her up to be arrested for drugs stashed in their car. In Will Robbins's 2009 novel *ICE*, the protagonist Woo comes from a fall, constantly negotiating with the streets, which is embodied in the characterization of the antagonist Ice. Ice is the drug dealer who runs the 'hood. His drug runners fear and loathe him. The young runners, including Woo, work hard throughout the story to overcome Ice. Conquering Ice is the rise; it is the equivalent to conquering the streets themselves. Conquering or surviving the streets is the overall theme of the genre of street lit. To balance the streets with life, we can say that conquering or surviving the streets is to make a success of one's life. This is the struggle that this genre depicts. It is the clarion call that it attempts to make.

In street-lit fiction, we see common storytelling devices at play: the protagonist triad, scenery as the primary stage, characters reconciling themselves with their environments (Buvala 2007). Except in fairy tales, some otherworldly kind of magic intervenes to aid characters' rise from poverty, ill health, or abusive relationships (Bottigheimer 2009). In the reality-based tales of street lit, we have urban dwellers who must conjure their own magic through their wit, savvy, and determination to overcome the streets by way of their will. In some stories, characters may have a mentor or a guardian voice, like Ms. Blue for Precious in the novel *Push* (1996); or three protagonists will serve as support mechanisms for one another. One good example of the protagonist triad is Anne, Isaiah, and Smoke in Terra Little's *Where There's Smoke* (2009). Mother, son, and father remind one another of past mistakes and present redemptions while the parents work to keep their son from succumbing to the lure of the streets.

Thus, the streets are the permanent antagonist of the genre. In this vein, the streets are never glorified or sensationalized. In street lit, the streets are the Pied Piper, the snake charmer of life. As such, it is something that we all must confront and deal with daily, as we use the streets as our major path through which we work, worship, play, live, and even die. In the street-lit genre, the streets are a transformational force. Its lure, whether embraced or denied, transforms characters through experience. Characters often descend into the netherworld of the streets only to reemerge wiser, more empowered, or more hopeful for a better life (Zimmer 2002).

4

THE DIVERSITY WITHIN STREET LIT
Themes and Subgenres

Before we can unpack the diversity within today's street literature, it is important to clarify how street lit is classified as a literary genre. Many educators (teachers and librarians), readers, authors, and publishers call street lit many things: ghetto lit, hip-hop fiction, and Triple Crown books (after the publisher), to name a few. However, the most common synonym for street lit tends to be the moniker "urban fiction." Admittedly, this is what I originally called street lit when I started working with the genre ten years ago. However, as I've researched this genre and its history, I learned something very important: street lit is not solely urban fiction, and urban fiction is not solely street lit. Also, street literature is just that: a body of works that as literature can come from both sides of the aisle—fiction and nonfiction.

Urban fiction is a literary genre of stories that are location specific to urban settings, as in city settings. If we look at a formal definition of *urban*, we can see that it indeed originates from, and is synonymous with, the term and idea of "city." From Merriam-Webster's online dictionary (at www.merriam-webster.com):

Main Entry: **ur·ban**

Pronunciation: \\'ər-bən\\

Function: *adjective*

Etymology: Latin *urbanus*, from *urbs* city

Date: 1619

: of, relating to, characteristic of, or constituting a city

Thus, urban fiction is an umbrella genre that contains a few subgenres, of which street lit is just one. Other urban fiction subgenres include chick lit and lad lit.

Chick lit is the female-focused genre that can be readily identified with stories such as the *Sex in the City* brand; the Gossip Girl series; *The Manny Files* (2006); and the progenitor of contemporary chick lit, *Bridget Jones's Diary* (1996) (Ferris and Young 2005).

Lad lit is a literary genre that speaks to male-focused comic stories that are often set in cities; the genre carries features similar to chick lit (Zernike 2004; Jones 2010). Leading authors of lad lit include Kyle Smith (whose 2004 novel *Love Monkey*, a male version of *Bridget Jones's Diary*, started the genre's popularity), Mil Millington, Eric Jerome Dickey, and Nick Hornby.

Notwithstanding the feminist underpinnings of chick lit and the male identity underpinnings of lad lit, when we look at all three genres—chick lit, lad lit, and street lit—it is their common urban backdrop that gathers them all into the genre of urban fiction. Urban fiction can be identified as an aspect of other genres, such as urban fantasy (e.g., Batman stories) and urban erotica (e.g., Zane).

Subgenres of urban fiction

The commonality of all urban fiction subgenres is the city setting. The difference between chick lit and lad lit, for example, when juxtaposed with street lit is socioeconomic standing—class. Most of the urban fiction subgenres are typically about characters living middle-class and upper-class urban lifestyles, whereas street lit is specifically about characters living low-income urban lifestyles. It is the socioeconomic condition of poverty that fuels much of the action in street lit. Chick lit and lad lit stories are set in "city central" or "center city" or "downtown," where metropolitan living is trendy and expensive, and characters are living the American dream. Street lit is set in "the 'hood" or "the ghetto" or "the inner city," where metropolitan living is anxiety ridden and survivalist. Nevertheless, the characters are American, and in their way, they are seeking the American dream, too. Living in a capitalistic society, consumerism is evident in the subgenres of urban fiction, regardless of socioeconomic status.

Street lit, chick lit, and lad lit have subgenres to them as well. Specifically, with chick lit, you will find diversity within the genre with further ethnic subgenres such as African American–focused stories, often referred to as sistah lit; Latina-focused stories, called chica lit; and Indian American stories, called Desi chick lit, to name a few.

Dad lit is a memoir genre (Warner 2007) that, though not a direct subgenre of lad lit, shows an across-the-aisle correlation between fictionalized and nonfiction men's stories.

WHAT'S DIVERSE ABOUT STREET LIT

Street literature today is diverse in the stories told because the genre in and of itself is about a location-specific city population that is indeed very diverse. Within street lit there are women's stories; men's stories; gay, lesbian, bisexual, transgender, and queer (GLBTQ) novels; and the very popular thug love. Additionally, there are many nonfiction works that can be considered contributions to street literature, as discussed in chapter 2.

It should also be noted that street literature is not a race- or culture-specific genre. Just as novels of yesteryear focused on the stories of low-income and working-class city dwellers who happened to be Irish (Crane's *Maggie*), Italian (Puzo's *The Fortunate Pilgrim*), and Jewish immigrants (Cahan's *Yekl*), street lit novels today focus on stories about city dwellers of the same socioeconomic status who happen to be multigenerational African American transplants from the South, as well as Latino, Caribbean, African, and Asian American immigrants (for examples, see Endy's 2007 *In My Hood*; Tash Hawthorne's *Karma with a Vengeance*, 2009; and Kia Dupree's *Damaged*, 2010). Some street-lit novels also depict the city experiences of whites, such as the character Molly in *Desperate Hoodwives* (2008), China in *Section 8* (2009), and even the character Skaggs in Paul Laurence Dunbar's *The Sport of the Gods* (1902).

Sister Souljah's novel *Midnight: A Gangster Love Story* (2008) provides perhaps the best illustration of the diversity of contemporary city neighborhoods. The protagonist, Midnight, is an African immigrant teen male whose family escapes Sudan under political pressure. The family arrives in America and finds a place to live in a predominantly African American Bedford-Stuyvesant community in Brooklyn. *Midnight* is a social narrative that also features Jewish and Asian merchants and families, Jamaican American artists, Amish rural farmers, and an inside look into Sudanese-Islamic immigrant family life. From *Midnight*, we get a rich picture of the multicultural tapestry interwoven in inner-city communities. In addition to cultural diversity within street lit, there is also gender diversity in the genre, with stories told from women's perspectives and men's perspectives, as well as a healthy contribution of GLBTQ titles.

MEN'S STORIES, WOMEN'S STORIES

This renaissance era of street lit entails men's and women's stories that are often dramatically romantic. Characters can be found working out relationship issues carried over from previous generations (e.g., absent parents, foster-care backgrounds) or a result of their immediate environment (e.g., single-parent households, being raised in poverty). Female characters are often portrayed as passionate and aggressively in love, focusing on their femininity in terms of their outward representations (e.g., grooming, name-brand clothing, social charisma). Male characters are typically portrayed as cool and detached, navigating various levels of masculine identity construction (e.g., community status, providing for family, social prowess).

The genre doesn't depict women as just hapless victims of their circumstances. Female protagonists are often proactive in seeking a better life for themselves and their children, even if at times their modes of operation are codependent on males or misdirected into climactic events (which actually is what is enticing about the novels—the drama). Female characters such as Winter in *The Coldest Winter Ever*, Gena in *True to the Game*, and Tionna in *Section 8* (2009), are often independent, confident, and resilient. Winter has an entrepreneurial bent to her that proves successful when she applies herself, Gena is a romantic poet who seeks to find meaning in the happenings of her life, and Tionna's loyalty and patience are capitalized by her resiliency to survive the streets and the drama it unfolds. Women's tales are often bildungsromans mixed with romance, coming-of-age stories in which the character goes through various trials and tribulations to arrive at a heightened sense of herself in the end. As is true in any literary genre, with some stories in street lit, characters are successful in the end, and some are not.

Male characters tend to be proactive in their quest for respect and credibility in their communities. Male characters are often go-getters (albeit sometimes illegally so) to provide material comforts for their families and often for the women they love. Part of the machismo exhibited in street-lit stories ascribes to ruthlessness applied to drug dealing and hustling and in navigating relationships with enemies, legal entities, mates, and family members. For example, the character Dutch in the Dutch trilogy is ruthless and unforgiving in his quest for not just neighborhood credibility but also respect from other mobsters he deals with in the established mafia. The male character Tech in K'wan's *Section 8* is characterized in the same way—an up-and-coming street hustler demanding and commanding respect from inside and outside of his 'hood.

Family respect is important in the portrayal of male protagonists as well. For example, Smoke in Terra Little's 2009 debut novel, *Where There's Smoke,* is an ex–street hustler turned high school teacher who learns he has a son. His biggest challenge in establishing a relationship with his wayward teen son is to keep him away from the lure of the streets. Another recent novel that illustrates African American males as seeking to make a better way for themselves is the 2009 Triple Crown novel *Ice,* by Will Robbins. In this story we learn that teen boys in the 'hood are striving for the same things as teen boys in any other community: to graduate high school, to go to college, to fall in love (not necessarily in that order). While working to graduate and go to college, Woo, the main character in *Ice,* has to also reconcile himself with the streets. With the help of his father, Woo maneuvers past the feared drug lord Ice to avoid being ensnared by a violent street life.

Male and female protagonists take on very human identity constructions that speak to realistic scenarios of surviving street life.

GLBTQ NOVELS

Early on in street lit's current renaissance (early 2000s), novels featuring GLBTQ characters were being published alongside mainstream titles such as *B-More Careful* (2001), *Let That Be the Reason* (2002), and *A Hustler's Wife* (2003). This subgenre is sometimes referred to as homo-thug novels by readers. The novels feature inner-city GLBTQ adult men and women (and sometimes teens) as protagonists. The stories often involve romantic entanglements that are sometimes graphic. Works such as Asante Kahari's *Homo Thug* (2004) depicts true-to-life stories of the struggles men have with spending long, lonely years in prison, where hormones and emotional needs are raging. In the novel *Wifebeater* (a double-entendre title) by Mister Mann Frisby (2005), there is a homo-thug character who marries the female protagonist while hiding his sexuality. Clarence Nero explores bisexuality in his acclaimed street novel *Three Sides to Every Story* (2006). In this urban drama

> Johnny meets James, a sassy, educated drag queen from the same side of the tracks, doing time for petty theft. Worlds collide when Johnny admits to his feelings for James and becomes torn between his long-repressed homosexuality and the woman and life he had before. (From the novel's back cover)

When James and Johnny are released from prison, part of their readaptation to society is reconciling personal and family relationships.

Convict's Candy (2006) by Damon Amin Meadows and Jason Poole is about the realities of prison life for a transitioning teen male who was convicted of fraud. In this novel, Candy is a transsexual on the brink of transitioning from male to female when she is convicted and sent to federal prison. While in prison she faces myriad relationship issues. The novel is also a social commentary on the state of HIV/AIDS in communities.

Another title worth mentioning that features a transgendered protagonist is A. C. Britt's *London Reign* (2007). *London Reign* features a teen protagonist who is a boy trapped in a girl's body. In this story, London is a serious street hustler who is also coming of age with her emerging sexuality.

There are quite a few street-lit novels that feature lesbian, bisexual, transgender, transsexual, and/or questioning characters. Some titles include *Love Lockdown* by Mia Edwards (2010), in which a secondary character, Rasheeda, is a powerful lesbian drug lord who, through the protagonist's half sister Tiffany, holds sway over the fate of the protagonist, Kanika. In *Dutch II: Angel's Revenge* by Teri Woods (2005), Angel is a ruthless lesbian who has a fair number of affairs to reach her criminal goals, whereas *Strapped* by Laurinda D. Brown (2007) features Monique Cummings, who adopts a masculine hustler identity in an effort to take control of her own life. Additionally, *Trickery* by Christine Racheal (2010) is about Taj, a lesbian sex performer who plays a dangerous game with her sexual identity that eventually reveals all her secrets. Of notable mention is the author N'Tyse, whose novel *My Secrets Your Lies* (2007) is an adventurous tale about a lesbian couple, Sand and Rene, who cut their teeth on the streets as hustling teens and grow as a couple into their own brand as adults. While Sand is seeking to legitimize her business, the long-term relationship begins to wane for Rene, who is questioning her gay identity. A major theme in the story is how Rene branches out to explore her identity in a heterosexual relationship.

All in all, GLBTQ novels follow the same conventions of the umbrella genre of street lit: surviving street life and navigating relationships. Although such titles may not be heavily populated within the overall street-lit genre, for interested readers (especially GLBTQ teens), this subgenre can serve as a gateway to a thriving GLBTQ literary genre that features authors like Clarence Nero and Laurinda D. Brown, as well as Michael Warren, Cheril Clarke, and E. Lynn Harris.

THUG-LOVE FICTION (WAHIDA CLARK)

Thug-love fiction is a subgenre of street literature in which author Wahida Clark dominates. With thug-love titles like *Thugs and the Women Who Love Them* (2004), *Every Thug Needs a Lady* (2006), *Thug Matrimony* (2008), *Thug Lovin'* (2009), and *Justify My Thug* (2011), Clark is the undisputed progenitor of this street-lit subgenre. She is a consistent *Essence* magazine best seller, and her novel *Every Thug Needs a Lady* appeared on the New York Times Best-Seller List shortly after its 2006 publication.

Although the traditional definition of *thug* is "criminal" or "gangster," within the context of street lit, there is a cultural (in terms of the streets) definition that is more about surviving street life than about being a criminal. The top definition at the website Urban Dictionary cites the rapper Tupac Shakur (1971–1996):

> As Tupac defined it, a thug is someone who is going through struggles, has gone through struggles, and continues to live day by day with nothing for them. That person is a thug. [A]nd the life they are living is the thug life. ("thyung" 2005)

Thus, being a thug is about how one successfully copes with intense daily life issues that are typically exacerbated by poverty and societal marginalities. Coming from an urban and decidedly hip-hop context, "thuggism" is about how one successfully copes with daily living on the streets. What is indicative of this subgenre, thug love, is how couples love and commit to each other (e.g., the infamous Clark characters, Trae and

Tasha) despite poverty and the perilous violence of the streets. Thug-love fiction directly focuses on the romantic and oftentimes erotic experiences of couples, and as such, it can be thought of as the romance subgenre of street lit. What differentiates thug-love fiction from traditional romance fiction is the grittiness of the stories and, again, the geographic common-ality of the streets as the staged backdrop for the stories' action. Another feature of thug-love fiction is commitment: Clark doesn't write one novel and the story is done. She writes her thug-love stories as a series, where characters' lives are deftly interwoven with one another to learn hard life lessons. Clark punctuates the point:

> Thugs do love and they can love hard. In *Thugs and the Women Who Love Them*, Faheem gave up his love of the drug game just to win Jaz's heart who was his real love. Yes, thugs do commit. Street running Trae and Kaylin married and fell deeply in love with Tasha and Angel. You reap what you sow or what goes around comes around is the underlying message in all of my books. You receive the reward or the punishment as a consequence of what you do. This makes my books, the "Thug Love" genre, different from Street Lit. (W. Clark, personal communication, June 9, 2010)

Clark's Thug Love series, currently in its fifth installment, begins with one set of characters in the first novel and then weaves to include and highlight friends of friends and foes in the subsequent books. If you are a loyal reader of the series, you become ensconced in the fictional world that Clark creates because you, as the reader, become invested in what happens with the characters. Case in point, one customer reviewer com-mented online at Amazon.com: "The magic of books 1–3 is the message that our [African American] powerful connections do exist (contrary to what the media would say) and that they are to be celebrated."

Payback Is a Mutha is a second emerging Clark series that is await-ing its third installment. This series approach has ensured Clark a loyal readership and plenty of space to develop characters that are very real, authentic, and true to life. In this vein, thug-love fiction maintains the very essence of street lit: keeping it real.

DIFFERENCE BETWEEN STREET LIT AND URBAN EROTICA

It is also fair to state that thug-love fiction is a bridge between street lit (in addition to authors already mentioned, think K'wan, Nikki Turner, Vickie

Stringer) and urban erotica (think authors such as Zane, Noire, Allison Hobbs). The two genres are often conflated with each other; however, it is important to understand that they are distinct literary traditions that oftentimes attract the same readers. Urban erotica is not location specific—its stories take place in settings from various geographies and socioeconomic loci. Thug-love fiction can almost be considered a blend of street lit and urban erotica, as it carries elements of both genres. Wahida Clark is pretty much in a class all her own, but other street-lit titles that come close to thug-love fiction include Noire's *Thug-a-Licious* (2006), Keisha Ervin's *Hold U Down* (2006), and even Teri Woods's True to the Game trilogy that chronicles the love saga of the infamous first couple of street lit, Gena and Quadir.

Today's street-literature stories have a central theme in common with street-lit stories of yesteryear: navigating relationships within the circumstances of poverty, where relationships are a primary lens to the story (i.e., from Charles Dickens's *Oliver Twist* to Sister Souljah's *The Coldest Winter Ever*). Street-literature stories, along the historical continuum, seem to focus on relationships with characters experiencing interpersonal conflicts (e.g., commitment, sexual identity) that they are seeking to navigate and overcome. Everyday citizens are characterized as having to reconcile unavoidable fates with street life and then struggling to either conquer or surrender to the will of the streets.

5

STREET-LIT READERS' ADVISORY
Expanding on the Patrons' Expertise

Readers' advisory for street literature requires the librarian to care about the genre, but more important to truly care about the patron. Reading is ultimately a private, personal endeavor. Thus, when patrons come to the library to seek a librarian's guidance on their reading interests, that interaction is intrinsically embedded with an immediate level of trust.

Because street lit is often regarded as transgressive and controversial, this trust factor is imperative for a successful readers' advisory interview between the patron seeking advisory on street lit and the librarian. Librarians must be aware and sensitive to the fact that when a patron, particularly patrons seeking this genre, come for professional assistance, the patrons are essentially the experts of their preference (i.e., they invariably know what they are looking for) and purposefully seeking the librarian's support. Thus, that support should be professional, which means it must be packaged within a nonjudgmental and open-minded attitude. Oftentimes patrons seek the librarian's professional assistance because they've acquired the reading habit from reading the genre and are seeking to read something more, something new. Patrons come to the librarian with the expectation that the librarian is knowledgeable about the genre and is competent (socially and intellectually) to recommend good, reputable titles, without rancor.

There are many people of all ages and backgrounds who read street literature; inner-city teens as well as suburban and rural teens read street literature. Many adults read the genre, including drug-rehab clients who may read street-lit novels as a form of bibliotherapy (Aiex 1993). I can attest to working with drug-rehab clients in Philadelphia and referring them to Donald Goines and Iceberg Slim novels for this purpose. Rehab clients may also enjoy novels by the authors K'wan, Relentless Aaron,

Vickie Stringer, and Teri Woods, to name a few. Just as teens have reported that they enjoy reading street lit because it teaches them what not to do (see Morris et al. 2006), adult readers who are rehabilitating from addictions they acquired from street living may read the genre for the same reason.

Because there is a significant teen readership of contemporary street literature, librarians must be attuned to adolescent developmental information needs that pertain to literacy activities that are text based as well as social (Chance 2008; Gorman and Suellentrop 2009). Teens' information needs are best met when the librarian exhibits respect for the teens' choices and encourages critical analysis as part of the teens' journey to becoming information literate. If a teen comes to a librarian asking to read *Section 8: A Hood Rat Novel* or *Thugs and the Women Who Love Them*, for example, it behooves the librarian to approach the query thoughtfully, considerately, and contritely. The librarian's regard for teen reading tastes and practices can significantly affect readers and determine their lifelong engagement with reading and with libraries.

Even though the reading patron may seek readers' advisory to learn what more is available in the library, it is not the librarians' place to shuffle the patron to other literary genres or other Black or Latino authors who may be more palatable to the librarian's personal reading tastes. It is also not advisable for the librarian to thoughtlessly whisk the patron to the "Black section" of the library to dismiss having to engage in the interview.

Librarians avoid becoming familiar with the street literature genre at their professional peril, as patrons are requesting it not just in urban public libraries but in all public libraries. It is best if librarians have an understanding of the genre from a historical perspective so that they are fortified with the understanding that the current iteration of the genre is cyclical, yet comparable to other fiction works that are now considered canonical (see chapter 2). To come to a well-rounded understanding of street literature as a genre, librarians need to approach the genre with respect for its historicity and cross-pollination of other genres.

SEARCH TERMS AND KEYWORDS

When embarking on a readers' advisory interview, librarians will often go to an Online Public Access Catalog (OPAC) or the Internet as their first point of access for searching for titles. In the earlier years of the street-lit renaissance (1998–2004), it was challenging to find the books in library catalogs because they were all categorized differently on the basis of location (e.g., "Baltimore (Md.)—Fiction") and ethnicity (e.g., "African Americans—Fiction"). During 2008 and 2009, I worked with the Library of Congress (LOC) to add "urban fiction" as an LOC subject heading (I. Quitana, personal communication, October 21, 2009). Thus, keywords and search terms that can be used for locating street lit via an OPAC include but are not limited to "urban fiction," with the following cross-references:

- gangsta lit
- ghetto lit
- hip-hop fiction
- street fiction
- street lit

Other LOC subject headings under which street-lit novels are cataloged include the following:

- inner cities
- street life
- urban life

All of these search terms can be used to search web resources such as LibraryThing (www.librarything.com), Goodreads (www.goodreads.com), and Shelfari (www.shelfari.com), where readers tag books they read and provide comments and reviews. Other tags to consider include the following:

- domestic fiction
- love stories
- bildungsromans
- urban lit

Although some street-lit titles are starting to be assigned the 650 MARC tag of "urban fiction," there is still a wide gap in finding street-lit novels that are correctly cataloged. Invariably, though, patrons will come into the library knowing the title of the book they are looking for. Often they will also know the author's name and the publishing brand (e.g., Triple Crown, Urban Books, GhettoHeat). One must keep in mind that many books are independently published or published by smaller publishing outlets. Thus, there are titles that may have the requisite ISBN but lack a full MARC record.

READERS' ADVISORY QUESTIONS

Questions that could be posed to patrons would be directed to the following access points: setting, story, relativity, authenticity. On the basis of these access points, when performing readers' advisory for street literature, questions that point to what appeals to readers include the following:

Setting

Q: IS THERE A PARTICULAR CITY OR 'HOOD YOU WANT TO READ ABOUT?

Street lit novels, as a location-specific genre, are often set in large metropolitan cities such as New York, Philadelphia, Oakland, Atlanta. Some novelists write stories about a particular region. For example:

- Teri Woods, Solomon Jones—Northeastern: Philadelphia
- K'wan, Relentless Aaron—Northeastern: New York City
- Kiki Swinson, Nikki Turner—Southern: Virginia, Baltimore, D.C.
- Quentin Carter, Keisha Ervin—Midwestern: Kansas City, St. Louis
- Renay Jackson—Western: Oakland

Patrons may want to travel to another location, or they may want to read about a familiar place. Either way, the librarian needs to be familiar with the geographical patterns of the genre, as the genre is setting focused and location specific.

Story

Q: DO YOU LIKE MYSTERIES? ROMANCE? FANTASY, SCI-FI, OR SPECULATIVE FICTION?

The genre features elements of other genres.

Mystery: For example, Teri Woods's novels are basically crime capers, so mystery readers would be interested in her works, as well as in Solomon Jones's titles such as *Ride or Die* (2005) and *C.R.E.A.M.* (2007).

Romance: Wahida Clark spearheads the thug-love genre, so readers interested in romance would enjoy her books, as well as Chunichi's Gangster Girl titles, which chronicle the love relationship between Ceazia and Vegas. Perhaps the most famous romantic couple in street lit is Gena and Quadir, the protagonists of the True to the Game trilogy by Teri Woods. Many street-lit novels' plots are centered on the romantic adventures and entanglements of young couples.

Speculative: Believe it or not, there are some literary fictions within the speculative fiction genre that are set in inner-city locations, like in street lit. Some titles include Zetta Elliott's *A Wish after Midnight* (2010), where Genna is a teen girl living in inner-city Brooklyn. She travels back in time to pre–Civil War Brooklyn with a schoolmate. Nalo Hopkinson's *Brown Girl in the Ring* (1998) is about a single mother Ti-Jeanne who is trying to survive in a volatile futuristic city environment while reconciling her latent supernatural gifts. Octavia Butler's *Mind of My Mind* (1977) is about Mary, who is born and raised in the 'hood. Her telepathic powers are so powerful that she is able to attract the best and brightest telepaths to render a war on their leader, Doro.

Street lit can be thought of as a blended genre that incorporates plot devices from various genres: romantic street-lit stories, mysterious street-lit stories, and stories that approach fantasy and science fiction.

Q. DO YOU LIKE ONGOING STORIES? SERIES?

Contemporary street lit has quite a few series that have garnered devoted fans. Some of the most popular series include the following:

- Desperate Hoodwives: Bentley Manor Tales by Meesha Mink and De'nesha Diamond
- The Bitch series by Deja King
- True to the Game trilogy by Teri Woods
- Thug Love series by Wahida Clark
- Wifey series by Kiki Swinson
- Gangster Girl series by Chunichi
- Hood Rat series by K'wan
- Flint series by Treasure Hernandez
- Dirty Red series by Vickie Stringer
- The Dutch trilogy by Kwame Teague
- The Cartel trilogy by Ashley and JaQuavis

Trilogies and series often attract teen readers, as they enjoy ongoing stories as a bridge to being able to read longer novels. Interest in series novels can support a teen's information literacy development by supporting the motivation to read and seeing a story to completion, coming to an understanding of layered character and plot development spanning a period of time, learning to discern good storytelling, and employing successful reading strategies that merit a joy for reading. Older teens enjoy reading series and trilogies as much as younger teens (Clark Cox 2008). Older teen patrons may appreciate a multivolume street-lit story that they can relate to.

Relativity

Q: DO YOU HAVE TO READ SOMETHING FOR A SCHOOL ASSIGNMENT?

This question is important for teen patrons who may have to read a novel for school. The librarian can still whet teens' appetite for street literature by referring them to canonical texts such as

- *Maggie: A Girl of the Streets* by Stephen Crane
- *Oliver Twist* by Charles Dickens
- *The Sport of the Gods* by Paul Laurence Dunbar
- *Native Son* by Richard Wright
- *The Street* by Ann Petry
- *Brown Girl, Brownstones* by Paule Marshall
- *Manchild of the Promised Land* by Claude Brown
- *The Autobiography of Malcolm X* by Malcolm X and Alex Haley
- *Down These Mean Streets* by Piri Thomas
- *Bodega Dreams* by Ernesto Quinonez

Teen patrons may come into the library asking for street-lit titles, and through the readers' advisory interview, it is possible to lead them to classic titles and contemporary literature that carry street-lit elements (e.g., *Moll Flanders* by Daniel Defoe, *Push* by Sapphire). A successful readers' advisory interaction occurs when a patron leaves with more than they anticipated on arrival at the library. With an open-minded, unbiased librarian, performing readers' advisory for street literature can actually be a means to promote information literacy and lifelong reading with teen and adult library patrons.

Authenticity

Q: SINCE YOU LIKE REALISTIC STORIES, WHAT ABOUT NONFICTION?
HOW ABOUT REALLY REAL STORIES?

This is an important question to ask because many believe that street literature is just fiction. This is not true. In fact, the nonfiction side of the genre is more prolific, with decades of documentation about the realities of living in inner-city neighborhoods. Some titles include the following:

- *Code of the Street: Decency, Violence and the Moral Life of the Inner City* by Elijah Anderson
- *We Beat the Street: How a Friendship Pact Led to Success* by Sampson Davis, George Jenkins, Rameck Hunt, and Sharon Draper
- *In Search of Respect: Selling Crack in El Barrio* by Philippe Bourgois
- *Random Family: Love, Drugs, Trouble, and Coming of Age in the Bronx* by Adrian Nicole LeBlanc
- *Gang Leader for a Day: A Rogue Sociologist Takes to the Streets* by Sudhir Venkatesh
- *The Corner: A Year in the Life of an Inner City Neighborhood* by David Simon and Edward Burns

There's also a wealth of memoirs and biographies that chronicle lives lived on the streets and that illustrate the intensities of low-income city living. Some titles include the following:

- *My Bloody Life: The Making of a Latin King* by Reymundo Sanchez
- *Monster: The Autobiography of a L.A. Gang Member* by Sanyika Shakur
- *Blue Rage, Black Redemption: A Memoir* by Tookie Williams
- *Lady Q: The Rise and Fall of a Latin Queen* by Reymundo Sanchez and Sonia Rodriguez
- *Project Girl* by Janet McDonald
- *Grace after Midnight: A Memoir* by Felicia "Snoop" Pearson
- *Our America: Life and Death on the Southside of Chicago* by LeAlan Jones and Lloyd Newman
- *Living at the Edge of the World: A Teenager's Survival in the Tunnels of Grand Central Station* by Tina S. and Jamie Pastor Bolnick
- *Makes Me Wanna Holler: A Young Black Man in America* by Nathan McCall

READERS' ADVISORY DISPLAY

Nonfiction titles could be coupled alongside similar fiction titles for an effective readers' advisory display.

Fiction	Biography/Memoir
Monster by Walter Dean Myers	*Monster: The Autobiography of a L.A. Gang Member* by Sanyika Shakur
A Project Chick by Nikki Turner	*Project Girl* by Janet McDonald
Dutch by Teri Woods	*My Bloody Life: The Making of Latin King* by Reymundo Sanchez
The Coldest Winter Ever by Sister Souljah	*Random Family: Love, Drugs, Trouble, and Coming of Age in the Bronx* by Adrian Nicole LeBlanc
ICE by Will Robbins	*The Autobiography of Malcolm X* by Malcolm X and Alex Haley

Librarians can also match street-lit novels with classic novels to challenge teen readers in the realm of information literacy. Teens could read two novels for comparison and to heighten their critical-thinking and analysis skills.

Contemporary	Classic
Push by Sapphire	*The Color Purple* by Alice Walker
Pipe Dreams by Solomon Jones	*Real Cool Killers* by Chester Himes
Midnight: A Gangster Love Story by Sister Souljah	*Manchild in the Promised Land* by Claude Brown
Bentley Manor Tales by Meesha Mink and De'nesha Diamond	*The Women of Brewster Place* by Gloria Naylor

Another idea for a readers' advisory display is to couple street-literature titles with movies available in the library.

Book	Movie
Black (2003)	*Jason's Lyric* (DVD—2000)
Dutch (2004)	*American Gangster* (2008)
The Cartel (2008)	*Blow* (2001)

Implications of Book Displays

Because the genre is largely one of leisure reading, I suggest presenting street-lit readers' advisory displays for summer reading programs and for Christmas holiday reading. Library displays during these times of the year coincide with extended school and vacation breaks for students and working adults. A street-lit display for Black History Month would be inappropriate because such a display would insinuate the genre as a monolithic genre, appealing to just one population of people, which it is not and does not. Such a display also inaccurately situates the genre in a vacuum, as if the genre has no other history, which is untrue (see chapter 2).

One effective display I saw in one of Westchester, New York's library locations had the genre in its own display case situated in front of the overall fiction collection. The librarian had featured titles merchandised on top of the display to attract patron attention. Other titles were arranged in a tiered flat formation to feature the covers. Signage was arranged to highlight the collection.

In my own professional practice, I used a rolling book cart to house and promote the street-lit collection. The main benefit of this display was for portability of the collection. The rolling cart was useful for helping patrons at the checkout counter and in other areas of the library for readers' advisory. Another advantage of the rolling book display was for when I had book club sessions for teen patrons: the cart made the genre easily available during book club meetings. Important features of the "urban fiction cart" (as it was called back then) were the following:

- Originally created genre labels for the books via a graphics editor
- Signage to identify the collection from near and far
- Checkout information posted right on the cart (e.g., no more than three books per patron at a time, maximum loan period of seven days)
- Portability of the cart to different areas of the library (e.g., adult fiction, young adult fiction, circulation and checkout, reference desk, programs)

Implications for Library Circulation

The readers' advisory display is a good way to couple current street-lit fiction with classic, literary fiction, nonfiction, and audiovisual titles. Patrons learn how the genre is situated within literary tradition and within the library space as a whole. A multiformat readers' advisory display (along with shorter, quicker borrowing periods as indicated earlier) may even deter the common high loss rate for street-lit novels because patrons get the opportunity to expand their view of the genre as it is connected to other books and materials. This might ignite an interest in patrons to try other titles and to return their book(s) to the library to read other items on display, which in turn can positively affect circulation. This is not a guaranteed approach, because patron communities respond to readers' advisory and outreach efforts in different ways. However, some kind of materials display for street literature is definitely a readers' advisory initiative that is worth the effort, time, and presentation.

Last, librarians should be aware of what is circulating and in high demand for their library. Street lit, even a decade into being on library bookshelves, is still a highly read and requested genre. Case in point, the Gary, Indiana, public library system had the following titles in the top ten of its top twenty hold list for May 2010 (Katterjohn 2010):

1   *Push* by Sapphire (A/YA)

5   *Wifey for Life* by Kiki Swinson (adult)

6   *Black Diamond* by Brittani Williams (adult)

8   *Payback* (Bluford High series) by Paul Langan (YA)

9   *16 on the Block* (Baby Girl Drama series) by Babygirl Daniels (YA)

These titles populate half of Gary's top ten titles on its hold list for this particular month. These data support the reality that library patrons eagerly read and request the street-lit genre. Thus, public library collections should provide access to requested and reviewed titles.

STREET-LITERATURE BOOK REVIEW RESOURCES

Librarians and teachers, by and large, do not want to censor or block access to reading materials that their patrons and students want to read. What often makes educators a barrier to reading materials is their lack of knowledge of credible book review resources for genres. For street lit, the following resources are important to know:

> *Library Journal*'s free electronic newsletter, *Booksmack!:* The newsletter publishes the monthly review column "Word on the Street Lit," by Rollie Welch, the librarian collection development manager

for the Cleveland, Ohio, public library system. He reviews between seven and ten titles per month, all prepublication street-lit titles. The column has been published on the Web since 2008—with a good search, you can find back entries by Rollie Welch and by Vanessa Irvin Morris. At present, Welch is the sole contributor to the column. To subscribe to *Booksmack!* you will need to go to the *Library Journal* website and click on the "Newsletters" link on the main menu.

Streetfiction.org website (http://streetfiction.org): This website is a premier resource for all things current in street literature, including book reviews, publication announcements, genre news, reader comments, and author interviews. Daniel Marcou, a corrections librarian, is founder and webmaster of this important resource. If you subscribe to the site, you will be emailed book blurbs and reviews as titles are posted on the site. Various announcements are posted at least twice a week. Titles are also available for purchase via the Streetfiction.org storefront on Amazon.com: http://astore.amazon.com/streetfiction-20.

StreetLiterature.com (www.streetliterature.com): Authored by myself, this blog features book trailers, book reviews, and commentary on the street-lit genre. Guest interviews and book reviews are consistently featured as well.

Admittedly, there are some street-lit review resources that situate the genre as an African American one. This may be a contextual categorization, as African American literature resources will feature all things African American, as will Latino resources and Desi resources, for example. Although review resources such as the African American Literature Book Club (www.aalbc.com) and Mosaic Books (www.mosaicbooks.com) may have reviews of street-lit titles, the reviews are layered deep within the site, as the genre is absorbed into African American literature. StreetLiterature .com, *Library Journal*'s "Word on the Street Lit," and Streetfiction.org are the only review sites, to date, that offer a cross section of themes that help define contemporary street literature as a city-focused genre as opposed to an ethnic-specific genre. Additionally, there are author and publisher websites for street literature (see the section "Street-Literature Publishers" at the end of this book).

However, the best resources for street-lit authors, titles, and trends are patrons. Patrons come off of the street into the library to read about the street. They bring their experiences and word-of-mouth expertise about what titles are hot and who the quality authors are. Getting good information from patrons requires that librarians trust the patron's insights and information. Librarians can follow up on that information to confirm and support title and author requests via professional book reviews from the resources cited here. In this social media age, information can be followed up via search engine mining, book retailer website tagging (e.g., Amazon .com, barnesandnoble.com, powells.com), Facebook author and publisher pages, and even Twitter lists and feeds.

THE LIBRARIAN'S STANCE FOR READERS' ADVISORY

The librarian's stance for readers' advisory for street lit requires the librarian to be fully engaged as a culturally sensitive information gatherer, qualifier, and researcher. A culturally sensitive and competent approach to readers' advisory for street literature requires the librarian to research the genre, to read the fiction and nonfiction, to understand its availability in various formats, and to situate the genre within literary tradition by making thematic connections between contemporary novels and literature of yesteryear. In this vein, the librarian then serves as an educator in that he or she presents and promotes the best that street lit has to offer, alongside established titles of similar story and characters. Above all, it behooves the librarian to listen, respect, and positively respond to his or her patrons' expertise about what they want to read.

6

TONING IT DOWN
Teen-Friendly Street Lit

Although many adults read urban fiction for entertainment, teen readers often consume these volumes not only as entertainment but also as an attempt to make sense of the confusion that permeates their communities. Living in poverty in America is a far cry from the mainstream, middle-class narrative depicted in the media (Barton and Hamilton 1998; Moje 2000; Compton-Lilly 2007). Outsiders to inner-city American life often struggle to accept that these fictionalized depictions of life in the 'hood could so closely parallel the daily realities that many Americans face; however, my fieldwork in teen readership of this genre confirms that street lit is largely based in a world that the readers recognize as real. As one book club reader, Angie (age sixteen), stated: "It's reality for me." Another clubber, eighteen-year-old Tanya, said: "It's all life; nonfiction, fiction. It's life." With American street-lit novels typically set in major metropolitan areas such as New York City, Atlanta, Los Angeles, Philadelphia, and Baltimore, teen readers often see themselves or someone they know (a friend or relative) within a narrative, and such recognition empowers them to make sense of their own lives (Morris et al. 2006).

> Indeed, as Lily Owens (1981, xiv) wrote in *The Complete Brothers Grimm Fairy Tales*, characters in oral fictions and folktales based on a parallel reality allow us to further understand the real: "however high or low, exaggerated or outlandish, the emotions and experiences of fairy-tale characters have their real-life counterparts. . . . [We are] recognizing our world in theirs."

There is a connection between the worlds depicted in street-lit novels and the worlds that inner-city teens navigate on a daily basis. Inner-city teens experience unique obstacles in their communities. Because teens are navigating these obstacles at the most intense developmental stage of their lives (adolescence), how they perceive their worlds is all the more intense and amplified (Anderson 1999; Dimitriadis 2003). To map the connection between the worlds of street lit and real-life ghetto worlds, it is necessary to place ourselves into the shoes of readers so that we may comprehend their localized narratives (Sumara 1996; Barton and Hamilton 1998). This may not be an easy or attractive option, as public educators (librarians and teachers) serving today's American inner-city citizenry often must accept that their students live and operate in the same raw and graphic conditions as the environments described in street-lit novels. However, such confrontation with the truth is necessary to document why teenagers living in inner-city communities gravitate so heavily toward stories that parallel their experiences rather than escaping into the polarized realities of other forms of literature.

It is necessary to note that the consumption of adult street lit by teen readers prompted cries of foul play from educators that the themes, language, and scenarios were too mature for young readers. Indeed, readers as young as twelve years old have been known to read novels like *The Coldest Winter Ever* and *Wifey*. However, it was street-lit authors themselves who spearheaded a softer, toned-down version of street lit for tweeners, thus igniting a much-needed publishing revolution for the African American and Latino young teen and tweener reading public. Specifically, teen-friendly street lit was started by the street-lit author KaShamba Williams.

TONING IT DOWN

During the spring of 2005, I attended an author event at the Overbrook Park Branch Library in Philadelphia, where the street-lit author KaShamba Williams was the featured guest, promoting her novels *Blinded* (2003), *Grimey* (2004), and *Driven* (2005). During the program Williams shared her story about her twelve-year-old daughter (at the time) wanting to read her novels, to which she replied, "Absolutely not." Williams conveyed that it was at that point that she realized the necessity of publishing a teen-friendly street-lit book for a younger reading audience. It was at that time that she announced the upcoming Platinum Teen series, in which to date four teen novels have been published: *Dymond in the Rough* (2005), *The Absolute Truth* (2005), *Runaway* (2006), and *Best Kept Secret* (2008). Author KaShamba Williams was the first author to publish a teen-friendly street-lit brand, with Precioustymes Entertainment Publishing (www.precioustymes.com). Williams's brand spearheaded an evolution in tweener publishing for inner-city tweener audiences, with authors such as L. Divine, the Kimani Tru conglomerate, Coe Booth, Paula Chase Hyman, and Kia Dupree realizing literary success.

THE INTENT OF TEEN-FRIENDLY STREET LIT

The intent of teen-friendly street lit is to offer the stories of inner-city living and struggle without the graphic language, violence, and sex scenes of adult street lit. The stories are primarily targeted at tweeners (twelve to fourteen) and younger teens (fourteen to sixteen). Although we can look to the ever-popular Bluford High series as well as established young adult authors such as Sharon Draper, Angela Johnson, Sharon Flake, Janet McDonald, and Walter Dean Myers, who have been writing teen-friendly urban novels with an inner-city focus for years, KaShamba Williams's Platinum Teen series signified a turn in young adult publishing for the urban, inner-city teen reading audience. What was significant about Williams's series was that the book covers displayed actual full-bodied pictures (not graphics, head shots, or silhouettes) of contemporary, relatable African American tweeners and teens, along with double-entendre titles that mirrored the representation of adult street lit. Also notable to Williams's series is that she literally branded the book covers as "teen-friendly street lit."

The works of Sharon Flake (*The Skin I'm In*, 1998; *Money Hungry*, 2001; *Begging for Change*, 2003) and Walter Dean Myers (*Monster*, 1999; *Autobiography of My Dead Brother*, 2005) are particularly important representations of young teen novels that chronicle realistic inner-city stories. We can definitely appreciate the artistry that Flake, Myers, and other African American tweener and young adult novelists exhibited in their works that garnered them literary awards such as the first Michael L. Printz Award for Myers's *Monster* and Flake's multiple Coretta Scott King Awards and honors. However, the Platinum Teen series was a refreshing contribution to YA literature because it was written in simple, straightforward dialectal language, laced with slang and contemporary terms that translated into fast-paced stories that tweeners and young teens readily related to. Tween readers enjoyed the sense of accomplishment of reading stories with characters that continued to evolve in installments, as opposed to novel story lines that were onetime reading experiences.

SALIENT TEEN-FRIENDLY SERIES

What ensured success of the teen-friendly street-lit series was the same entrepreneurial approach that engineered the success of adult street lit —self-publishing and packaging (or branding). KaShamba Williams self-published the Platinum Teen series and packaged it with colorful, photographic book covers and double-entrendre titles. By offering installment stories instead of stand-alone novels, along with realistic, relatable stories, more African American–focused teen-friendly street-lit series emerged with significant readership:

> Drama High series is spearheaded by L. Divine (2006–ongoing) and
> is currently at fourteen volumes. Set in California, the series
> focuses on the teen protagonist Jayd Jackson, who navigates her
> life between the ghetto of Compton, California, and attending
> high school in a white Los Angeles suburb. Divine engages with
> her teen readers via her MySpace page, where she regularly adds
> updates on her writing process and responds to reader questions.
> The series target audience is age fourteen and up.

> Denim Diaries series, by Darrien Lee, boasts four volumes with
> more to come. Lee is an *Essence* magazine best-selling author
> of adult street-lit novels. The series chronicles the teen coming
> of age of protagonist, sixteen-year-old Denim Mitchell. We
> follow Denim's roller-coaster life as she and her diverse group
> of friends experience first loves, school drama, and increased
> responsibilities at home and beyond. Lee does a good job
> balancing the issues of the streets with realistic parental
> presence. The series, which attracts boy and girl readers alike
> (as well as their parents), is nicely packaged with attractive
> photographic book covers (www.denimdiaries.com).

> Bluford High series (repackaged) was originally published by
> Townsend Press in 2002, with artistic drawings of African
> American characters as the book covers. In 2006, Townsend
> partnered with Scholastic Press to reissue and repackage the
> series with contemporary photographic book covers depicting
> African American teens. It is believed that the Bluford series was
> repackaged to bring the series into the discourse of the modern
> street-lit movement. Townsend engages with Bluford readers
> via a Facebook page, where it updates readers on upcoming
> titles, answers questions, and moderates discussions on a reader

discussion board. The Bluford High series target audience is middle school tweeners, ages twelve to fourteen.

Kimani Tru series (2006–ongoing) was originally independently published, with eleven volumes published in 2007 alone. However, since 2007, the series has been an imprint of Harlequin Books (www.eharlequin.com/store.html?cid=590), with twelve additional volumes. Kimani Tru books are written by a variety of writers, with authors Monica McKayhan and Earl Sewell being frequent contributors. Kimani Tru titles are geared toward readers between the ages of sixteen and twenty.

Fab Life series is very popular with older African American teen girls and is suitable for school library collections. Penned by Nikki Carter, titles include *Not a Good Look* and *All the Wrong Moves*.

So for Real series is another popular series by Nikki Carter. This series is targeted at middle school–age readers. Titles include *Cool Like That*, *It's All Good*, *Step to This*, and *It Is What It Is*.

Ni Ni Simone series, in which author Ni Ni Simone publishes a series that focuses on teen experience of inner-city living. Her characterizations are a good balance between the serious issues and the normal teen angst that inner-city teens face, offering insight on relationships, self-esteem, and body image issues with an optimistic view of everyday life. Simone also interweaves her characters throughout the installments, where different stories from the same neighborhood are featured in various titles. Simone maintains an active Facebook fan page, where she regularly engages with her teen readers. Boasting almost five hundred followers, on the page Simone responds to comments, questions, and other contributions from teen readers all over the world. Teens communicate about their reading experiences, their favorite characters, and how they have acquired a love of reading from reading her books. One teen posted on the site in 2010: "ive read all the books, and ive hated reading but ever since i read your books ive loved reading lols."

Teen-friendly street-lit series ushered in a movement in YA publishing to meet the reading interests and needs of urban African American tweeners and younger teens. As we've discussed in this book, however, street lit is not just an African American genre (see chapter 2). It is important to note, though, that had it not been for street lit and its current interpretation of African American inner-city life, YA publishing would not have experienced the renaissance for African American–focused series fiction that it has, which filled the much-needed gap in literary series for African American teen readers.

CHRISTIAN TEEN-FRIENDLY SERIES

A further outcome of teen-friendly street lit is the emergence of Christian-themed series for the urban African American teen reading audience. There are quite a few Christian-focused teen-friendly series for urban African American teen readers. These titles are often geared toward the 12–14 and 14–16 age groups. Stephanie Perry Moore is perhaps the most prolific of the Christian series writers. Her titles include the following:

Beta Gamma Pi series (ages 14–16)

Carmen Browne series (ages 12–14)

Yasmin Peace series (ages 12–14)

Payton Skyy series (ages 14–16)

Perry Skyy, Jr., series (ages 14–16)

ReShonda Tate Billingsley writes the Good Girlz series (ages 14–16), Victoria Christopher Murray heads the Divas series (ages 14–16), and Jacquelin Thomas pens the Divine and the Divine and Friends series (ages 14–16).

These Christian series are often set in urban settings with African American teen characters navigating home life, social romances, and personal struggles that are resolved with prayer and application of religious principles. These series also fill an important gap in Christian teen fiction. Whereas YA literature was respite with works such as the Left Behind series (sixteen volumes) by Tim LaHaye and Jerry B. Jenkins and the Diary of a Teenage Girl series (multiple iterations: *Caitlin*, *Maya*, *Chloe*, *Kim*) by Melody Carlson, it was definitely missing an African American presence within this literary tradition. The emergence of street lit inspired a (re)turn to African American–focused Christian fiction as an alternative to tweeners and young teens reading adult-oriented street lit.

As we all know, literature comes in various textures and flavors to meet the reading interests and needs of all kinds of readers. Readers have degrees of sensitivities, from reading graphic stories like horror or supernatural fiction to reading sexy stories like urban erotica (e.g., Zane) and contemporary romance. In teen-friendly street lit, the same holds true: there are tweeners and teens who are sensitive to reading teen-friendly street lit, and there are older teens who are able to handle A/YA street lit.

Teen-friendly street-lit novels, series, and the Christian works are not meant to act as censorial substitutes for contemporary A/YA street lit. There will be teens whose sensitivities and interests will lean toward teen-friendly street lit, and there will be teens who will request contemporary A/YA street lit. Both audiences should be equally respected with an ample collection to meet their reading and information interests and needs.

It is understood that school media centers tend to have more rigid collection development policies. Teen-friendly street lit can be a great compromise for developing middle and high school collections with compliant street-lit stories. Authors such as Coe Booth, Paula Chase Hyman, Todd Strasser, Paul Volponi, Alan Sitomer, and Allison van Diepen offer teen-friendly street-lit novels that would be appropriate for both public and school library collections. Classic works that have stood the test of time and critique (e.g., *Manchild of the Promised Land*, *The Coldest Winter Ever*) are good additions to a high school library collection. Nonfiction memoirs and biographies, such as *The Autobiography of Malcolm X*, are valuable additions also.

"KINDA SORTA BUT NOT STREET LIT" YA WORKS

There are a few authors who write novels that are teen friendly and set in urban contexts that may appeal to readers who have exhausted your collection. The following authors have debut novels at the time of this writing that have received good response from readers and educators. Trustfully, these authors will continue to write for the YA audience:

> Zetta Elliott's *A Wish after Midnight* (2010) is a speculative fiction novel about fifteen-year-old Genna, an Afro-Latina from the Brooklyn projects who unexpectedly goes on a time-travel adventure to her same neighborhood during the U.S. Civil War. The novel is historically accurate and has received good reviews for being an engaging read.

> Tachelle Wilke's *Amanda's Ray* (2010) is a teen-friendly urban narrative about Amanda, a talented writer and lyricist, who is starstruck by a female rap star and wants to be just like her. An unfortunate event lands Amanda in a juvenile detention center,

where she goes through a downward identity crisis because of her obsession with contacting her celebrity muse. Amanda eventually comes full circle to realize that the real star is herself; all she has to do is look within. Readers have lauded this novel as an inspirational read.

Dia Reeve's debut novel *Bleeding Violet* (2010) can be considered a dark fantasy novel for the A/YA reader, ages sixteen and up. Sixteen-year-old Hanna is a biracial girl who tries to reconnect with her mother who abandoned her. To be able to stay in her mother's home, Hanna must settle in with new friends at the local high school. This is not an easy feat for a manic-depressive girl who experiences hallucinations. However, given the haunted nature of the town she is living in, Hanna learns that her unusual, sometimes violent nature is quite compatible with the paranormal weirdness of this new community. She is quickly recruited by a demon hunting group and goes on a quest to save the town from dark evils. This novel can be considered a hybrid of horror and mystery—it has sex, violence, and some gore.

Thug-love queen Wahida Clark started the YA imprint Wahida Clark Presents Young Adult in early 2011, with the debut of Rashawn Hughes's novel *Under Pressure.* The narrative features Quentin Banks, who is comfortable with his swagger on the streets of the Bronx. Eventually, "QB" spends some time in prison, but on release he returns to his Bronx neighborhood to do some good in the world. A little older and much wiser, QB becomes a youth counselor at a local teen community center. He mentors two young men at the center, Torry and Chase. When a showdown targeting QB for an old beef occurs, he struggles to quell his instinct for revenge. *Under Pressure* is a coming-of-age story that may appeal to teen male readers. Warning: there are some graphic elements in the novel that may be too mature for readers younger than sixteen years old. It is anticipated that Clark will continue building her YA brand such that it will be milder in content, to appeal to a wider range of teen readers.

THE VALUE OF TEENS READING STREET LIT

Because the ghetto is the inner city teen's primary world, I contend that even before inner-city children reach their teenage years, most are profoundly aware of their environments. Having worked with inner-city teens for nearly a decade (and having grown up as one myself), I have seen how street lit aids in teens' overall comprehension of their surroundings. These teens of the hip-hop generation have learned to combine both urban literature (street lit) and music (hip-hop) to empower themselves. Looking at life critically to "know what's going on" is key to today's teens' survival, and street lit plays an important role in not only heightening their resistance to any unsavory people and locations surrounding them but also strengthening their resiliencies, thus allowing them to carve out a sober space within their neighborhoods.

Street lit provides many benefits to its teen readership, bringing value to their worlds and points of view. As my fieldwork has revealed, teen readers regularly incorporate the novels' themes into their daily responses to their environment, in hopes of learning what not to do (Morris et al. 2006). To coin Kenneth Burke's phrase, as cited by Elizabeth Long (2003, 131) in *Book Clubs: Women and the Uses of Reading in Everyday Life*, teens use street lit as "equipment for living." Thus, although the books may not be written for that specific purpose, teenage book club members show that teens often interpret the novels as cautionary tales, and the more of the genre they read, the more critical they become of their future readings as well.

Consistent reading of the genre is creating an outcome of inner-city teen readers gaining critical analysis skills about both their own reading tastes and, by extension, heightened understanding of their communities. Because adults predominantly write street-lit novels, I posit that these authors are reporting back to their cultural communities to document their experiences into history and to offer warning of the perils of bad choices regardless of one's environment. With these novels, the authors are seeking a reinscription from their readers, by which readers are affirming the authors, and the authors are thus reconciled from their wounds of the past. To perceive street-lit books as acts of contrition illustrates an ongoing conversation and a mutual inscriptional discourse between author and reader (Iser 1978; Rosenblatt 1983; Appleyard 1991; Sumara 1996). New beginnings occur when you remember the past and the present and bring both into the future (Lavenne, Renard, and Tollet 2005; Hua 2006). This chaotic process creates opportunities to move the African American ghetto culture and community forward. Although some insiders and outsiders to inner-city living may not endorse the lifestyles depicted in the dramatic scenarios of street-lit novels, it is important to recognize the genre's effect on students, including one fourteen-year-old ninth grader who wrote in a teen survey I conducted in 2008, "[For teens] there are a lot of things going on in the world and we need to be involved."

Because the teenage years mean that a child is in the process of articulating his or her identity, and because inner-city students must often navigate the added stress of their intense and unpredictable communities, I submit that inner-city teens crave the validation that street literature provides because reading the stories suggests that they can gain control of normalized anxieties and uncertainties and make changes in various aspects of their beliefs and understandings.

Reading street lit allows teens to claim some modicum of ownership over their daily lives by being able to compare their realities and identities to the characters in these folk stories. Street lit gives its teen readers a sense of proaction, allowing them to slow down, to examine and process the rise and pitfalls of ghetto life. By taking their time to contemplate the world in which they live, as readers the teens have a chance to decide, "This is not *me*; these are just the circumstances of my life right now. This is just my current world, my current reality, but it is not the reality I want to live."

7

"WHO PUT THIS BOOK ON THE SHELF?"
Street-Lit Collection Development

In this chapter, we look at ways to create a basic foundational street-lit collection that can evolve and grow as new authors and titles are published. The chapter discusses common collection development issues that have arisen with this genre because of library behaviors of the reader and librarian. I identify the classics of the genre, the most popular series publications, and characteristics of the genre's format that can indicate whether a title or author is worth consideration for a street-lit collection. I also discuss street lit, in its full identity as "street literature," which by its designation as a body of literature confers consideration and inclusion of nonfiction titles such as biographies or memoirs and poetry. Last, I explain collection development, management, and promotion strategies for the purpose of prolonging the shelf life of a genre that is not as heavily circulated as it is heavily appropriated by its reading community.

CIRCULATION AND CENSORSHIP ISSUES

Since the 1999 publication of *The Coldest Winter Ever*, street-lit fiction has been flying off library bookshelves across the nation. Because of the popular nature of the genre, novels are voluminously checked out with a low rate of return. Circulation rates for major street-lit titles show that libraries own many copies, with a low amount of copies available on the shelves, compared to many copies being checked out, along with phantom copies that are "lost" or "missing" (see table 1). Table 1 illustrates that, although a library may own many copies, titles not only are often not readily available at library locations not only because they are lost or missing as a result of patron behavior but also may be unavailable for checkout because of library processing, cataloging, or they are stuck in transit between library locations. Either way, the deeper meaning of table 1 conveys that, by and large, across the country street lit is heavily owned by libraries but not necessarily consistently available. Libraries often do not get full circulation (i.e., a book that is checked out is consequently checked back in to the library) on street-lit novels because readers may borrow the books from the library and then pass them along to other readers; a common pattern is for the book(s) to get lost within a networked web of readers sharing one title.

TABLE 1
Circulation cross section of large public libraries on August 3, 2010

Library System	Push by Sapphire	The Coldest Winter Ever by Sister Souljah	Queen Bitch— Bitch series, part 4
South Durham (NC) County Library	*45 copies* 17 checked out 9 unavailable 19 available	*29 copies* 8 checked out 7 unavailable 14 available	*0 copies*
Northeast Free Library of Philadelphia	*205 copies* 112 checked out 15 unavailable 78 available	*82 copies* 34 checked out 32 unavailable 16 available	*13 copies* 4 checked out 9 unavailable 0 available
West Los Angeles Public Library	*225 copies* 45 checked out 11 unavailable 169 available	*51 copies* 15 checked out 4 unavailable 32 available	*7 copies* 1 checked out 6 unavailable 0 available
Midwest Chicago Public Library	*463 copies* 142 checked out 144 unavailable 177 available	*133 copies* 54 checked out 63 unavailable 16 available	*69 copies* 42 checked out 16 unavailable 11 available

Titles chosen on the basis of *Essence* magazine's latest (at time of writing) Bestsellers Book List (October 2009). "Unavailable" status means the book is lost, missing, damaged, in cataloging, on hold, or otherwise unavailable for checkout. The total picture of what unavailable means would be to add the number of checked-out copies to the number of unavailable copies.

STREET-LIT SEX, THE LIBRARIAN, AND CENSORSHIP

Another issue with developing a circulating collection for street lit is the genre's racy content and determining how appropriate the genre can be for a library's collection in a given community. Some titles are more sexually and violently explicit than others (this is also true for the romance, thriller, and horror genres) and may not be appropriate for more conservative communities and readers. It is the issue of sexual explicitness (not to be confused with urban erotica) that often prompts librarian censorship of street lit. On the basis of formal and informal field interviews and blog comments from urban and suburban public service librarians, librarians have been known to not process street lit for addition to library shelves, to hide street-lit novels and graphic novels in reference desk drawers, and/or to merchandize street lit in locked display cases.

A diplomatic approach to balance this censorship issue is for librarians to first consider titles that come recommended from established professional and scholarly resources (i.e., book review lists, professional columns, and articles in print and on the Web). Thus, if any challenges arise for a street-lit title, the librarian has professional documentation and scholarship to support the material. (Note: My field research shows many teachers and librarians admitting to confiscating [teachers] or censoring [librarians] street-lit books. However, to date, there appears to be no documentation of street-lit novels being formally challenged and/or banned, by parents or other community stakeholders, from library shelves.)

The most important consideration when developing a street-fiction collection is that the cream rises to the top, with librarians providing the best representation of the genre as possible. As in any other literary genre, street fiction has its classics, its must-haves, and it has its shelf sitters, so to speak. Librarians can discern which is which by becoming active readers of the genre and by employing effective professional protocols for determining appropriate titles. Such protocols would include paying attention to new publications from established street-lit publishing outlets, purchasing established authors, and reading credible book reviews.

SEPARATING THE WHEAT FROM THE CHAFF OF STREET FICTION

In this current renaissance of street literature, there are "classic" titles that are requisite for any reputable collection, and then there are criteria to consider when choosing must-haves for a well-rounded collection. Classic titles of street fiction are classic because they set the bar for the prolific nature of the genre and have remained standard-bearers for readership since their publication. Street lit is also known for its prolific series titles—many stories are published with cliff-hangers, promising sequels, trilogies, and full multivolume series. Some titles are trilogies, whereas some series are beyond six-volume installments and can virtually claim their own library shelf.

THE CLASSICS

Although these titles are not all-inclusive, I do believe few would find it hard to dispute this canonical list for current-day street lit:

> *The Coldest Winter Ever*—Sister Souljah
> *True to the Game*—Teri Woods
> *Flyy Girl*—Omar Tyree
> *B-More Careful*—Shannon Holmes
> *Let That Be the Reason*—Vickie Stringer
> *Push*—Sapphire
> *Gangsta'*—K'wan Foye
> *Push*—Relentless Aaron
> *Black: A Street Tale*—Tracy Brown
> *Thugs and the Women Who Love Them*—Wahida Clark
> *Dutch*—Teri Woods/Kwame Teague
> *A Hustler's Wife*—Nikki Turner

These titles are representative of the genre as a whole because, by and large, these authors have established themselves as writers and publishers of quality titles after a decade or more into the renaissance era of this genre.

There are a few salient reasons I believe these titles and authors set the bar for the street-lit genre:

1. The titles all tell street tales that are candid, realistic, and uncompromising in characterizations and plot developments that exhibit a tension between characters and their relationship to their surroundings, thus contributing to the naturalist style of American literary tradition.

2. The realism of the stories makes an immediate impact on readers, and that impact continues beyond the book to focus on the author him- or herself and the author's subsequent contributions to the genre (e.g., readers waited patiently for eight years for Sister Souljah's next book after *The Coldest Winter Ever*).

3. All of these titles were the debut novel of their authors, yet affected the reading public such that many of the books became best sellers (whether they were best sellers on the street (particularly Relentless Aaron and Teri Woods) via media outlets such as the *Essence* magazine and Urban Books best-seller lists (i.e., *True to the Game, Let That Be the Reason, A Hustler's Wife*) or via the New York Times Best-Seller List (i.e., *The Coldest Winter Ever* and *Flyy Girl*). Furthermore, most of the authors on this canonical list started in the genre as entrepreneurs, literally hustling their books on the street.

Teri Woods is credited as spearheading the entrepreneurial aspect of the street-lit genre, which remains the backbone of the genre's success as a literary force. During the late 1990s, Woods peddled her books on 125th Street in New York City, selling more than one hundred thousand copies on her own, alone. Author Relentless Aaron also sold more than one hundred thousand copies of his books before signing with a mainstream publisher (St. Martin's Press). Woods remains a contributing pioneer of the genre; she continues to write and publish as an author (via Grand Central Publishing), and she continues to independently publish up-and-coming authors (via her independent publishing house, Teri Woods Publishing), whereas Aaron has moved his work into video and film production (R. Aaron, personal communication, August 3, 2010). Authors such as K'wan continue to promote their novels on the streets, wishing to keep a close connection with their readers (K'wan's Twitter feed, July 2010).

SERIALIZING STREET FICTION

Street fiction boasts quite a few highly regarded series that undoubtedly need to be included in a solid street-fiction collection. Deja King's Bitch series (with five installments) is probably the most popular street-fiction series and, as such, has maintained its popularity over the years. However, some communities may balk at the series' title. Thus, aside from King's series, other important trilogies and series include but are not limited to

Around the Way Girls, various authors, volumes 1–7 (as of July 2010)

Girls from the Hood, various authors, volumes 1–5 (as of September 2009)

The Cartel trilogy—Ashley and JaQuavis
- *The Cartel*—1
- *The Cartel: Tale of the Murda Mamas*—2
- *The Cartel: The Last Chapter*—3

Bentley Manor Tales—Meesha Mink and De'nesha Diamond
- *Desperate Hoodwives: A Bentley Manor Tale*
- *Shameless Hoodwives: A Bentley Manor Tale*
- *The Hood Life: A Bentley Manor Tale*

True to the Game trilogy—Teri Woods
- *True to the Game*—part 1
- *True to the Game: Gena*—part 2
- *True to the Game: Qadir*—part 3

Dutch trilogy—Teri Woods and Kwame Teague
- *Dutch*
- *Dutch II—Angel's Revenge*
- *Dutch III—The Finale* (Teague)
- *Dutch III—International Gangster* (Woods)

Flyy Girl trilogy—Omar Tyree
- *Flyy Girl*—part 1
- *For the Love of Money*—part 2
- *Boss Lady*—part 3

Thug Love series—Wahida Clark
- *Thugs and the Women Who Love Them*
- *Every Thug Needs a Lady*
- *Thug Matrimony*
- *Thug Lovin'*
- *Justify My Thug*

Wifey series—Kiki Swinson
- *Wifey*—part 1
- *I'm Still Wifey*—part 2
- *Life after Wifey*—part 3
- *Still Wifey Material*—part 4
- *Wifey 4 Life*—part 5

Flint series—Treasure Hernandez
- *Choosing Sides*—book 1

- *Working Girls*—book 2
- *Back to the Streets*—book 3
- *Resurrection*—book 4
- *Back to the Hood*—book 5
- *A King Is Born*—book 6
- *The Finale*—book 7

An investment into purchasing these series titles can contribute to a circulating street-fiction collection in virtually any public library that is responsive to the street-lit readership community. The series are valuable for street-fiction collection development because the varied stories provide a pluralistic view of the genre and the inner-city culture it illustrates. The power of the serialization of street fiction is illustrated through a collection of stories that

cover varied regions of the United States, thus representing various dialects, slang terms, and locations

provide a healthy mix of women's and men's stories, as well as multicultural stories (e.g., Latino, African American, GLBTQ)

offer a stable representation of established authors who have a significant readership and fan base, and thus a high percentage of readers know about these titles and/or authors

attract readers to the collection because of known authors, creative titles, and relatable book covers

CHARACTERISTICS OF REPUTABLE STREET-FICTION NOVELS

In addition to the classics and series titles, a well-rounded street-fiction collection would include titles that invariably feature the following characteristics:

- Written in Standard American English, with authentic language (African American, Latino, or regional dialect, lingo, and slang— SAE is a sanctioned academic assignation for Standard American English, as is AAVE for African American Vernacular English)
- Authored by established writers who have published consistently reputable titles in the genre, including but not limited to

  Relentless Aaron

  Mark Anthony

  Wahida Clark

> K'wan Foye
>
> Erick S. Gray
>
> Shannon Holmes
>
> Deja King (also Joy King)
>
> Sister Souljah
>
> Vickie Stringer
>
> T. Styles
>
> Nikki Turner
>
> Teri Woods

- Authored by up-and-coming, must-read authors who may be referred by patrons, colleagues, book review resources, and street book vendors. Such must-read writers include but are not limited to:

> Ashley and JaQuavis (a literary team of two authors, Ashley Snell and JaQuavis Coleman)—*New York Times* best seller as of November 2009 for *The Cartel—2*, part of The Cartel trilogy
>
> Deborah Cardona, also penned as Sexy (Latina protagonist novels: *Chained, Two Fold,* and *A Better Touch*)
>
> Chunichi (notables: Gangster Girl series)
>
> Darren Coleman (notables: *A Taste of Honey* and *Before I Let Go*)
>
> Keisha Ervin (notables: *Hold U Down, Chyna Black, Mina's Joint*)
>
> Terra Little (notables: *Where's There's Smoke* and *Where's There's Smoke 2*)
>
> J. Love (notables: *Heavy in the Game* and *The Game Don't Wait*)
>
> Jeff Rivera (notable: *Forever My Lady*)
>
> T. Styles (notables: *A Hustler's Son* and *Miss Wayne and the Queens of DC*)
>
> Kwame Teague a.k.a. Dutch (notables: *Dutch III—The Finale* and *Thug Politics*)
>
> KaShamba Williams (notables: *Blinded, Grimey,* and *Driven*)

- Packaged preferably in slightly oversized paperback format (tends to be the most popular and preferred format) with a colorful, attractive cover and catchy title, usually indicative of street lingo (e.g., *Diary of a Street Diva, Street Dreams, Gunmetal Black*)

- Published by established publishing outlets, including the following:

  Triple Crown Publications

  Melodrama Publishing

  Urban Books

  Grand Central Publishing

  Dafina imprint = Kensington Books

  St. Martin's Press imprint = St. Martin's Griffin

  GhettoHeat Publications

  Simon and Schuster imprint = Atria/Strebor Books

  Q-Boro Books

- Reviewed by credible review sources such as the following:

  Library Journal's "Word on the Street Lit" column (go to libraryjournal.com, enter "word on the street lit" in the search box)

  Streetfiction.org: www.streetfiction.org

  Urban Reviews Online: www.urbanreviewsonline.com

  Street Lit Review: www.streetlitreview.com

  StreetLiterature.com: www.streetliterature.com

  The Urban Book Source: www.theurbanbooksource.com (URL for book reviews: www.theurbanbooksource.com/ bookreviews.html)

Having said all that, it must be noted that contemporary street lit has a strong entrepreneurial bent that the library world must respect. Patrons will often come into the library suggesting or asking for titles that they saw on street-vendor tables outside the library's doors. It is important that librarians take an engaged approach to locating relevant titles that may not be readily available via traditional library book vendors.

STREET-LIT NONFICTION

There are many important titles in the nonfiction collection that depict the real-life survival stories of American inner-city citizens. These books are nonfiction biographies, memoirs, poetry, and some research materials. Notably, there has been considerable socioanthropological and ethnographic research works published parallel to the street-lit renaissance novels that tell the stories of citizens surviving street life in various ways. Some salient titles include the following:

- Biographies or Memoirs

    A Question of Freedom: A Memoir of Learning, Survival, and Coming of Age in Prison by R. Dwayne Betts (2009)

    The House on Childress Street: A Memoir by Kenji Jasper (2006)

    Grace after Midnight: A Memoir by Felicia "Snoop" Pearson (2007)

    From Pieces to Weight: Once upon a Time in Southside Queens by 50 Cent (2005)

    E.A.R.L.: The Autobiography of DMX by DMX and Smokey D. Fontaine (2003)

    War of the Bloods in My Veins: A Street Soldier's March toward Redemption by DeShaun "Jiwe" Morris (2008)

    Makes Me Wanna Holler by Nathan McCall (1994)

    Project Girl by Janet McDonald (2000)

    I Choose to Stay: A Black Teacher Refuses to Desert the Inner City by Salome Thomas-El with Cecil Murphey (2003)

    Fist, Stick, Knife, Gun: A Personal History of Violence in America by Geoffrey Canada (1995)

    My Bloody Life: The Making of a Latin King by Reymundo Sanchez (2000)

    Living at the Edge of the World: A Teenager's Survival in the Tunnels of Grand Central Station by Tina S. and Jamie Pastor Bolnick (2000)

- Socioanthropological Ethnographies (Documentary Research)

    Crackhouse: Notes from the End of the Line by Terry Williams (1993)

    Rosa Lee: A Mother and Her Family in Urban America by Leon Dash (1997)

    Our America: Life and Death on the Southside of Chicago by LeAlan Jones and Lloyd Newman (1998)

    Code of the Street: Decency, Violence and the Moral Life of the Inner City by Elijah Anderson (1999)

    In Search of Respect: Selling Crack in El Barrio by Philippe Bourgois (2002)

Random Family: Love, Drugs, Trouble, and Coming of Age in the Bronx by Adrian Nicole LeBlanc (2003)

Gang Leader for a Day: A Rogue Sociologist Takes to the Streets by Sudhir Venkatesh (2008)

Lady Q: The Rise and Fall of a Latin Queen by Reymundo Sanchez and Sonia Rodriguez (2008)

Righteous Dopefiend by Philippe Bourgois (2009)

Grand Central Winter: Stories from the Street by Lee Stringer (2010)

- Poetry

  Close to Death: Poems by Patricia Smith (1998)

  The Rose That Grew from Concrete by Tupac Shakur (1999)

  Bum Rush the Page: A Def Poetry Slam edited by Tony Medina and Louis Reyes Rivera, foreword by Sonia Sanchez (2001)

  Speak the Unspeakable by Jessica Holter (2003)

  The Moments, the Minutes, the Hours: The Poetry of Jill Scott by Jill Scott (2005)

  The Dead Emcee Scrolls: The Lost Teachings of Hip Hop by Saul Williams (2006)

  Street Love by Walter Dean Myers (2006)

  Please by Jericho Brown (2008)

NONFICTION AND FICTION ALONG THE HISTORIC CONTINUUM

The publication years for the nonfiction street-lit titles parallel the renaissance period for fiction street-lit titles, circa 1999 to the present day. It is important to note that, although authors began to tell their stories via fiction, researchers and literary writers were also publishing the same kinds of nonfiction stories at the same time. This parallel timeline connects to the historical literary continuum of the emergence of the naturalist literary movement at the turn of the nineteenth century into the twentieth century (1880s–1940s). Authors like Stephen Crane, Mario Puzo, and Abraham Cahan published street-lit novels depicting the realistic, raw, and gritty tales of Irish, Italian, and Jewish immigrants living in inner-city enclaves at the turn of the twentieth century. Richard Wright, Ann Petry, and Chester Himes extended the naturalist literary movement into African American literary tradition with their street-lit stories depicting the harsh realities of American Blacks' uneasy adjustment to city life during the Great Northern Migration (circa 1910–1970)—notably, Paul Laurence Dunbar's *The Sport of the Gods* (1902) was an early contribution to the naturalist movement within African American literary tradition. During the civil rights era, street-lit fiction and nonfiction classics such as Claude Brown's novel *Manchild of the Promised Land* (1965) and Malcolm X's autobiography, *The Autobiography of Malcolm X* (1965) continued the realism and naturalism strain in storytelling of the inner-city Black experience. Donald Goines and Iceberg Slim carried the style with their raw, pulp-fiction street-lit novels of the 1970s. At the turn of the twenty-first century, we have American Black and Hispanic or Latino American authors like Sister Souljah and Jeff Rivera alongside Reymundo Sanchez and Jessica Holter telling their tales of daily living in inner-city enclaves from both sides of the aisle, fiction and nonfiction, just as in yesteryear, with novelists being published at the same time that street literature in the form of broadsides, pamphlets, and chapbooks were circulating and being sold on the streets (Shepard 1973). The streets always have stories to tell, real stories about the people who live in urban ghettos. Rapper and actor Ice-T said it best in his foreword to Iceberg Slim's last published novel, *Doomfox* (1998, ix): "Change the conditions of the ghetto, and the stories will change." A Philadelphia teen street-lit book club member once said, "It's all real. Fiction, nonfiction. It's all the same. It's life. It's all real." Indeed.

COLLECTION DEVELOPMENT STRATEGIES

Street fiction's popularity has overwhelmed public libraries such that the demand is sometimes beyond what a library can supply. Thus, many libraries contend with a high theft rate of street fiction—books are abundantly checked out but have a low return rate. There are a few strategies that can be employed that can lower the theft rate and incentivize return of the books for full circulation of the material. Techniques that I, and other librarians, have employed include the following:

- Allow a maximum number of titles per patron (suggested maximum of three).
    - Readers read the books quickly. When teens were asked how long it takes for them to read a street-lit novel, they reported "sometimes a day," "less than a week" (Morris

et al. 2006). Because of this, instead of one patron check-ing out a stack of six to a dozen titles at one time, allow patrons to check out just three titles that they must return on a seven-day loan.

- Circulate street-lit collections on a seven-day loan.

    Readers read the books quickly, and if they have another two weeks (or longer) to return the books, it is during this window of time that they may loan the book to another reader and then another and ultimately the book is lost in a web of readers—degrees of separation away from the original borrower of the book. If readers read the book within the first week of checking it out of the library, they are more apt to remember that the book is due at the library and will return it on time.

- Interfile—mix it up.

    Interfile street fiction with the rest of the fiction collection to heighten the patron's exposure to more of the library's fiction collection; this also lets readers know that street fiction doesn't sit outside or beyond other literary fiction works. Keep street fiction within literary tradition on the shelves.

    If there is really high demand for the genre, a cluster collection could be arranged at the beginning of the fiction collection, especially if your fiction collection is arranged by genre. Highlight the street-fiction collection alongside romance or mystery so that patrons experience browsing through the street lit as a part of a wider range of materials.

    Combine fiction and nonfiction titles as a cluster collection. This could be a good book display for summer reading, Christmas vacation reading, spring break reading, and to promote author events. A combined fiction and nonfiction collection shows that the genre is to be taken seriously, as both fiction and nonfiction often depict similar reality-based narratives.

- Make the cluster collection portable.

    One librarian reported situating a small cluster collection of street lit alongside the computer sign-up station of the li-brary because that is where patrons focused their energies on entering the library. This heightened exposure of the materials and consequently increased checkout of books.

Another librarian reported creating a cluster collection on a small book cart so patrons could take the cart where they were sitting in the library to browse the collection. This invariably increased the number of books the patron wanted to check out. This strategy also increased readers' advisory interactions between patron and librarian.

Another librarian stationed a small "What's Hot!" collection right on her desk so that she could keep track of what was being checked out, what needed to be shelved, and what needed to be reordered.

One librarian kept multiple copies of classic street-fiction titles specifically as an outreach collection that she took with her and booktalked when she visited local high schools. When she got down to one copy of a title, that title be-came "reference" (i.e., noncirculating) within the traveling outreach collection. She then booktalked the reference copy to encourage students to come to the library to get a circulating copy that was on library shelves. Having clas-sic titles provided students with titles they already knew; thus, they were empowered and engaged in the booktalk as experts of the genre. This in turn opened up space for the students to give suggestions to the librarian of hot, new titles and authors that she could add to her street-lit collection. Students invariably visited the library after a school visit to browse the in-house circulating collection, because after the readers' advisory interaction at school, they then felt confident to enter and browse the library.

- Combine the old with the new.

    Put a "classic" label on what I like to call the big three of street lit, *The Coldest Winter Ever*, *Flyy Girl*, and *True to the Game*, and shelve them in your classics collection alongside George Steinbeck and Mary Shelley, Mark Twain and Leo Tolstoy, Alice Walker and Richard Wright.

    Put a "street-lit" label on important street-literature works such as *The Autobiography of Malcolm X* by Malcolm X and Alex Haley, *The Street* by Ann Petry, and *The Real Cool Killers* by Chester Himes and shelve them alongside

KaShamba Williams and Relentless Aaron, Kiki Swinson and Chunichi, Shannon Holmes and K'wan Foye.

- Listen to your patrons.

  Readers will tell you what new titles are coming out or what titles you may be missing from an author or series, and they may inform you of entrepreneurial authors who may be accessible for adding to your collection. Case in point, patrons introduced me to *The Coldest Winter Ever*, *Push*, *True to the Game*, *Flyy Girl*, and *B-More Careful* a decade ago when the street-lit renaissance began to take form. It was patrons who also told me about the Kiki Swinson *Wifey* series, and it was the same teen patrons who told me to stop reading *Wifey* and check out *Jane Eyre*—yes, that *Jane Eyre*.

STRATEGY RESULTS

These strategies have been executed by frontline public librarians and have proved effective with the following outcomes:

- Increase shelf life of a circulating street-lit collection by ten weeks
- Introduce readers to a wider range of literary works that fit into the same genre
- Increase readers' advisory conversations that have been educational for both the patron and the librarian
- Aid the positive return rate of borrowed materials back into the collection

Of course, these strategies are not etched in stone. Try one, or combine one with another, incorporating all strategies with an active discourse with your patrons, doing what is best for your community. Some of these methods may seem unconventional in their approach and application; however, they have been executed successfully in working American public libraries located in inner-city neighborhoods, without any challenges from the community or other stakeholders. These strategies emphasize our educative mission and goals as public education servants while enhancing our abilities to do just that—serve.

8

CHARACTERS OUTSIDE THE COVER
Who and What Are We Reading in the Library?

Inside the library, the librarian, the reader, and the authors of library materials are all in conversation with one another. The librarian maintains and promotes the collection, readers inquire and use the collection, and authors are the conduits through which collections are built because they create the materials housed in libraries (e.g., books, movies, music). Thus, in looking at street lit within a library context, we must take into account how librarians, readers, and authors read and respond to the genre and to one another. This is important to explore because it is through books that we interact with one another as readers. As librarians, we must always be cognizant of who we are when we do what we do and with whom we do it with.

THE LITERATE LIBRARIAN

I have established in this book the librarian's position not as an informa-tion expert who is an outsider to the community but as a patron of his or her own service library and service community, and thus an insider to the community. As such, the librarian is a reader of the library, the collection, the patron, and most of all of him- or herself as a community member and advocate. Indeed, as a reader of multiple figured worlds that inter-sect, interweave, and inform one upon the other, the librarian is a constant lifelong learner of the human condition via his or her social interactions in the form of the reference and readers' advisory interview (Bartlett and Holland 2002). This multilayered figured world encompasses the librar-ian's world of information retrieval, storage, management, social interac-tion, and cultural literacy practices. As such, the librarian, as a de facto reader of genre, is a representation of the notion every reader for every book, per S. R. Ranganathan's law of library science: "every reader his or her book."

For example, for librarians who serve an inner-city community, their sociocultural literacy is expressed in the way they navigate their own interactions in the streets. In the 'hood, everyone is a reader: a reader of text, moods, tonalities, the weather, and the streets themselves. The inner-city librarian (and teacher for that matter) is not exempt from this genus of information literacy.

It is not unheard of that inner-city public librarians witness and/or experience some of the themes laid out in street lit. A case in point, I myself have witnessed threats and harassment in the library, drug overdoses in the library, sexual activity in the library, riots in the library, robbery of the library, even death in the library.

As an inner-city librarian, I've also witnessed children becoming "A" students because of time spent in the library; teens changing from delinquents to college students or military personnel because of their consistent involvement with reading, library programming, and staff; adults empowered to navigate bureaucratic city systems because of information or contacts obtained from the library; and on many occasions, people of all ages obtaining a lifelong reading habit because of their relationship with the library.

Truth be told, both the dark side and the bright side of public librarianship parallel similar themes laid out in various ways in the street-lit genre. There are regularly scenes in street-lit stories where characters enact in literacy activities that include reading books; writing letters, poems, and lyrics; and doing research at the public library. Thus, it behooves us as librarians to be literate about our patrons' literature, because invariably we are also characters in the very stories they read and in the very stories they live.

THE EXPERT READER

In turn, when we think about the themes and plots of street lit, we see true-to-life stories about a day in the life of the 'hood, where people may be experiencing employment challenges, struggling to navigate the educational process, participating in livelihoods supported by an underground economy, emoting intense personal relationships, and too many times dying at the hands of someone's gun. Additionally, name-brand labels, cars, and accessories are detailed in the stories to create a vivid picture of what characters are wearing, driving, and consuming as citizens of a capitalistic society. Amid the chaos of walking the streets, interacting in relationships, finding jobs, going to school, and experiencing various levels of violence, characters are portrayed as looking very expensive. Aside from the materialistic bent, these same street-lit narratives offer up stories about young people working hard to rebuke the lure of the streets; families facing challenges head-on and succeeding; men and women loving, living, and learning life lessons in relationships. Be it fiction or nonfiction, street lit tells stories from a spectrum of human experiences. Street lit illustrates how low-income Americans are in just as hot pursuit of the American dream as their wealthier fellow citizens who live just as chaotic and disorganized lifestyles in suburban and upper-class enclaves (e.g., The Real Housewives series on Bravo). Canonical literature (e.g., Crane's *Maggie*, Puzo's *The Godfather*, Fitzgerald's *The Great Gatsby*) reminds us that daily living has nothing to do with how much money a person earns, the color of one's skin, or the ethnicity of one's culture; it has everything to do with ways in which we seek to identify with and qualify for the consumerist, capitalistic, hegemonic culture called the American Dream. Contemporary street lit embraces this same distinction.

When readers read such themes and plots over and over again, book after book (which they do), such reading ignites their imagination such that they are able to locate themselves in the context of the stories (Doyle 2005; Morris et al. 2006). Dennis Sumara (1996) advises us that when we read, we respond to the text on the basis of the social and cultural context in which the reading occurs. In my work with the Widener Teen Book Club (2005–2008), I found this to be very true. How the teens were reading street lit when they were seventh graders was very different from how they were reading it as tenth graders. Case in point, during their middle school years, book clubbers responded to the genre with comments like, "It teaches what not to do," "It's ghetto fabulous!" However, by the time they were high schoolers (thus a little older, thus having experienced more things and read more things) their responses were more intricate and included analysis from a wider lens. For example, during one book club meeting when I asked the members if they had read Kiki Swinson's *Wifey* (2004), a book clubber named Sharon waved her hand dismissively and said, "That interfered with my Jane Eyre."

This kind of reader response shows that readers, no matter who they are, do not read in a vacuum. I posit that it is actually nearly impossible to do so. Thus, Sharon's response was based on a full field of experience, which included the canonical text *Jane Eyre*. Interestingly enough, Sharon was not alone. In response to her statement, another book clubber, I'll call her Deena, chimed in and exclaimed something like, "You read that? Gurl, that was good, wasn't it?" Sharon and Deena then began a side conversation about the interesting drama of *Jane Eyre*.

You might be saying, "Nah, this is impossible—this is not true." However, I am here to say that the teens' holistic response is in line with reader response theory that talks about how readers pull on a repertoire of life experience and bring those expectations to the texts they choose to read (Iser 1978; Sumara 1996). Just by the act of reading in and of itself, there is an "indeterminacy filling" that occurs when the imagination is invoked (Sumara 1996, 31). The indeterminate gap between the imagination and lived reality is filled when we read text, creating heightened thinking by the reader, because the reader, by virtue of reading, has to synthesize what is being read with what is being lived. Thus, when inner-city citizens read street lit, their imaginations re-create the stories' worlds inside their minds, which in turn they synthesize with their personal reality (comparison and contrasting of identities and situations between the book and the reader), thus filling the gap between the imagination and reality. Wolfgang Iser (1978) calls this filled gap a new world; a virtual text; a heightened, new sense of how oneself "fits" into one's own lived world. It is about "making the familiar strange," "transcending the particular," negotiating and constructing reality via narrative (Bruner 1986, 13, 159).

It is within this indeterminate gap that the reader has space to evaluate, assess, and make meaning of what they read to add to what they already know and to learn and process what they do not know. It is this gap, during the act of reading, whether as an insider to the story or not, where the lifelong learner lies. Through reading, readers either are learning more about themselves personally or are learning more about humanity as a whole. Either way, the act of reading adds to the reader's repertoire as a human being living a human experience (Iser 1978).

Just the pure act of reading street lit validates the reality of urban inner-city life for those living it, because the stories connect the fantastical (the drama and trauma of ghetto life) with narratives that convey, "Yes, this exists; yes this is real." This validation empowers the reader to be open to negotiating the reading of their personal worlds, with an entry into synthesis, analysis, and evaluation of their environment, the people in it, as well as their own location and interaction within their lived world. In street lit, the streets signify their stories back to the people of the streets.

This is powerful stuff. Street lit has the potential to affect readers in ways that can challenge their worldview, because the pure act of reading ignites a revelatory connection between what was previously viewed (or read) as scary, confusing, or even as entertainment to a critical lens of personal interpretation. Once this bridge has been made, readers' worldview broadens and they then ask critical and nuanced questions like the following, from an Amazon.com post on *Thug Lovin'*, part 4, from June 26, 2010:

> Why take such a loved character and have him beat his wife to the point where he doesn't know how she got on the floor?
>
> Are you kidding me? What is that and what was the point of reducing them to that level? Don't devoted readers of the series deserve better than that?

This kind of critical analysis is prevalent among reader comments and reviews on Amazon.com for many street-lit titles. Brooks and Savage (2009, 52) conducted a study on Amazon.com reader comments for street literature and learned that "the appeal of Street Lit narratives derives, at least in part, from readers' perceptions of literary quality (e.g., characters, storyline, theme) as well as the writer's ability to depict a reality that resonates with her readership (e.g., 'this book is how it is on the street')." We can see how the act of reading, regardless of what is being read, organically prompts readers to naturally synthesize and assess what they read. With street lit, these acts of literacy manifest as book club discourse, book networking and sharing between friends (and in social media, with authors, too), and commenting and reviewing books on book review websites and blogs). Decidedly, through these various acts of reading and information literacy practices, critical analysis becomes a natural part of the reading of the reader's world.

THE ACTIVE AUTHOR

The authors of street lit are for the most part from the streets of which they write. "[Some] Street Lit authors are ex-convicts and recovering drug addicts who began writing while in prison and rehab centers. Their personal experience with the life and culture they describe, adds realism to their gritty, raw stories" (Morris et al. 2006, 18). There are also street-lit authors who write stories based on what they've lived and witnessed as working-class residents of inner-city communities. Last, as in any other literary genre, there are also authors who may have never personally experienced their stories but write them because they want stories that have long been "swept under the rug" to be told (see Teri Woods's foreword in this book).

Because many street-lit authors are from the 'hood that they write about, readers who are from the 'hood have immediate entry into the novels, because the language, tone, settings, and characters are recognizable and relatable. The novel itself is like a cultural artifact between the author and reader that establishes an understanding that the story exists and that the story will be told and heard. This relationship is strengthened by the fact that the author has written a story and the reader is imaginarily living that story by virtue of reading it. Both intentions are iterative and interactive when the reader reads the book. Therefore, when the reader decides to go past the cover and the title, the choice alone to read the content of the book infers that the reader trusts the author's intent. As each page is read, that trust is further invested so that the reader can engage in the story.

Although this trust of authorial intent may not have been the impetus for street-lit authors to write (after considerable reading and research of this genre, I posit that many authors write to be heard, to claim voice to the reading of their own worlds), this trust is an implicit covenant for readers. In an inner-city world where it can be challenging to maintain faith in stability or consistency, because of the precarious vibe of confusion, chaos, violation, and/or assault, to be able to trust what one reads within the ignited hermeneutic imagination of the environment of a street-lit novel is pivotal for readers. Pointedly, for inner-city teens, to read narratives that play out the dramas that they "read" in their everyday lives without them having to suffer the repercussions, wounds, or consequences of those dramas serves as cautionary reconciliation of "Yes, this is life in the 'hood," and "Been there, done that, I don't have to go out like that" (meaning, "I don't have to end up like that" or "That doesn't have to be me"). Just as contemporary young adult fiction helps teens make sense and meaning of their worlds, street lit serves the same purpose for teens (and adults also) living in the same settings as the stories.

The author writes the book to talk to the reader, and once the book is written, the author then becomes a reader of the book as well. The reader listens to the author by reading the text. However, there is a dialogue here. Street lit is so popular that with or without a librarian's readers' advisory, readers read street-lit novels in common, sharing their readings and the books among themselves (Morris et al. 2006). Eileen Landay (2004) tells us that reading fiction and biographies engages dialogue within oneself (the author to him- or herself and the reader to him- or herself), between the reader and the author, and when text is shared between different readers. In all these realms, street lit is a powerful conduit for readers finding an authentic voice within an American culture that otherwise keeps them marginalized and therefore silenced. Where there was possibly no previous relatable voice in mainstream literature for inner-city readers, readers and writers felt this void and cried, "No!" They found a voice from their own streets to write and document their own culture. The street-lit author Shannon Holmes (2005, 3) said:

> The experience and quality that I bring to my writing can't be bought, faked, or learned in school. . . . [R]eaders know that I know what I know. . . . Through my novels, I invite the readers to journey with me into the streets. Come see what I've seen. . . . Let me show the gritty and grimy undercarriage of society. The side that some in the working class don't acknowledge or are unaware of.

Street lit gives voice to the voiceless, be they author or reader. Street lit is a gritty, sometimes harsh, but always uncompromising shout from the streets transcribed into written text, to be reread and retold to the imagination, thus bridging lived reality with the reality of the mind, validating the truth of one's existence. That said, street lit is necessary for all readers who are exposed to the genre because it informs them that they are literate readers of their own lived worlds and that they have a voice and place not just in living but also in assessing and critiquing their American reality.

THE READING LIBRARIAN

In this vein, librarians must be readers of not just street lit but as much literature as possible that rounds out the literary environment in which street lit thrives. This means that librarians must be familiar with African American literary tradition (e.g., Chester Himes, James Baldwin, Zora Neale Hurston, Walter Mosley, Octavia Butler, Samuel Delaney, Edwidge Danticat, Toure, to name a few), Latino literary tradition (e.g., Pam Munoz Ryan, Sandra Cisneros, Junot Diaz, Piri Thomas, Cristina Garcia, Julia Alvarez, to name a few), chick lit (which can be considered urban and women's fiction), lad lit, GLBTQ literature, and contemporary fictions that depict urban settings (e.g., James Patterson, Zetta Elliott, E. Lynn Harris, Janet Evanovich, Tananarive Due, to name a few). Librarians must also remember that cultural literary traditions are diasporic in scope. Thus,

African American literature is not just stories about the streets or Black people in America, but the genre also can encompass Caribbean, African, and Black European and Canadian stories. The same is true of Latino literature, chick lit, and GLBTQ literature. For street lit encompasses myriad genre spaces—African American and Latino American experiences, gendered stories, and urban fictional narratives that are historical and contemporary, local and global.

When we as librarians are open-minded lifelong readers and learners via reflexivity and inquiry into our own professional practices and reading repertoires, we are that much more fortified to engage patrons in full readers' advisory interviews. It's not only a matter of the librarian knowing many genres for the sake of being able to tell the patron, "We have this and we have that," but such a repertoire is vital so that the librarian can parse out from the patron the depths of the patron's literary repertoire, to open up space to considering a fuller range of literary compatibilities and possibilities in what the patron wants to read.

9

HUSTLIN' STREET LIT
Pushin' Books and Programs

Many creative strategies can be applied to marketing and programming for street lit. Some of these promotional ideas include book displays, book clubs, field trips, and other literacy events. Some of the programming ideas are transferable between school and public library settings.

I see three main purposes for promoting street lit in the form of library programming: (1) to engage reluctant readers, (2) to promote the genre within the literary context of the library collection, and (3) to market the library as a community space for interactions and conversations that arise from reading street-lit materials.

It is important to plan programming around street lit to support reading and learning for reluctant readers who may find entry into reading the genre because its writing style is often representative of everyday, relatable language, dialect, and lingo. By promoting the genre's literariness across literary categories and formats by way of connecting fiction with nonfiction, books with DVDs, poetry with music, and canonical texts with contemporary texts, the library makes a statement that supports equitable access to texts that may serve as cultural artifacts. Engaging library patrons in reading circles or book clubs that read street lit helps educate readers about one another's ideas in response to reading various stories with various representations.

BOOK DISPLAYS

Book displays can be a very effective programming strategy in which the genre intersects with multiple literary formats. By setting up a book display that features titles of various reading levels and formats, readers from diverse perspectives may be attracted to the display, which can result in increased browsing of the library collection and heightened circulation of library materials.

For example, when I was librarian at a Philadelphia branch location, I created a portable book display cart of street-lit titles. This display cart was rolled into the meeting room to sit alongside me as I facilitated weekly teen book club meetings. Teen patrons would attend the meeting and peruse the cart. Invariably, they checked out books from the cart.

Book displays placed at the entry of the fiction area, such as the one in the Westchester library that I described in chapter 5, can serve as an effective enticement. The first thing patrons see on display is the street-lit collection, which can serve as a gateway to exploring the rest of the fiction collection.

For outreach purposes, street-lit titles can be displayed as part of a booktalking repertoire for the librarian. You are almost guaranteed rapt attention when you booktalk street-lit novels to city teens, particularly when you couple book titles with music titles. For example, librarians can suggest that if patrons like a particular book, they might like a certain song:

Title and Author	Song and Artist
Road Dawgz by K'wan	"Rough Riders Anthem" by DMX
True to the Game by Teri Woods	"Other Side of the Game" by Erykah Badu
Stackin' Paper by Joy King	"For the Money" by Fabulous and Nicki Minaj
The Cartel by Ashley and JaQuavis	"How I Got Over" by the Roots
Heavy in the Game by J Love	"Over" by Drake

As discussed in chapters 4 and 5, you can combine texts from other genres along with movie titles to create a book display that is rich in coverage and depth.

BOOK CLUBS

Forming a book club around this genre is probably the most effective way to engage library patrons into reading street lit and embracing the reading habit as a vital part of one's lifelong learning modus operandi. The genre seems to excite and motivate readers to talk about what they read and why they read street lit (Sweeney 2010). A browsing of street-lit titles on Amazon.com affirms the point that readers are experts of this genre. Reader comments on popular titles on Amazon.com often generate further reader response that is often rich in critical analysis. Many reader comments on the street-lit pages of Amazon.com exhibit a wide reading repertoire (Brooks and Savage 2009).

Because of the prolific publishing nature of the genre, I have found that readers often want to read and discuss multiple titles during book club meetings. With teenagers, the developmental needs of self-definition and meaningful participation bolster their internal assets of commitment to learning and positive values when they are able to choose their own titles to read and then actively discuss those titles in a book club setting (Alessio 2004; Gorman and Suellentrop 2009). Teens feel ownership and responsibility for the discourse and outcome of the book club. This aids in their emerging life skills of self-sufficiency and personal responsibility. Although multiple titles may sound like a confusing approach for a book club discussion, I have found it to be a requested approach for teen and adult readers alike. There is something empowering, I believe, for readers when they have a choice as to what to read rather than being prescribed one particular title, on the basis of a librarian's or teacher's supposed expertise. Because readers often have experiential entry into the genre's stories, they are immediate experts of the genre's content and context. Thus, reader-driven title selection for the group is an important strategy for a successful book club. Although a multiple-title approach allows for exposure and discussion to more books within the genre, a downside to the method is that readers may feel they are missing full engagement into a story they hadn't personally read. It is best, however, for book club members (teens and adults alike) to take ownership of the group structure and agenda so that opportunities for critically understanding what works and what does not work in a reading group become fodder for establishing a unique, workable identity for that group.

ADULT AND YOUNG ADULT BOOK CLUBS

I have worked with teens and adults in book club settings focusing on street lit for more than five years. Book club discourse gives library patrons space to critically discuss street-lit stories. Book club meetings facilitated by a librarian or other educator offer readers the opportunity to unpack various representations in the stories; to pull up characterizations, plots, and themes; and to problematize them for the purpose of deepening personal understandings about community, personal identity, and how one can further construct their identity.

Working with teen library patrons who read street lit is important because their engagement with a reading community that is discussing literature critically further opens up opportunities for more literacy activities such as the following:

- Collective authorship

    In the teen book club I facilitated from 2005 to 2008, the group ultimately moved from talking about street-lit stories to collaboratively writing a street-lit story. Before the group disbanded in 2008, they had worked up character outlines for protagonists and antagonists and a chapter-by-chapter outline that each book club member took on and wrote him- or herself. The plot outline totaled nine chapters.

- Writing poetry and journaling

    I have seen success with both teen girls and boys with using poetry and self-reflective journaling as a parallel exploration of street lit. In the book club meetings, members would bring poems they liked, would read poems from the street-lit novels (e.g., *True to the Game*, *Black*, and *Upstate*), and would share poetry they wrote during the book club and from their MySpace pages and Facebook notes.

- Artwork

    Out of respect for gender-specific adolescent developmental needs, I had success alternating weekly book club sessions, scheduling sessions for boys only and for girls only. I have found that this is an important strategy to employ with adolescents because, after a while, they need time to have conversations in a single-sex setting to be able to say things and think about things they don't yet feel safe doing in a coed situation (particularly boys). In this vein, I have sat with teen boys and watched them produce beautiful artwork as they talked freely about street life, street stories, and their strategies for living in an inner-city community. This outcome is reminiscent of bibliotherapy, where talk about books and stories produces a reflective stance that can be healing.

- Self-esteem activities

> These activities invariably engaged teen girls where they would talk about street-lit stories and then question their own self-esteem against female characters in the books. Girls would consider, "Is this me?" or challenge the character: "Why did she do that? Why did she put up with that?" This kind of critical inquiry resulted in craft activities where teen girls wrote affirmations on heart-shaped cutouts; created collages from magazines; or reaffirmed one another through group talk, during which they would give one another advice and support about their personal lives.

These outcomes illustrate how engagement in a genre that is oftentimes considered controversial or lowbrow can garner impactful literary and literacy-related results that are multimodal. Through various book club activities we learn that urban teens are engaged in a wide array literacy activities that are print based as well as online. Of course, these strategies can work successfully with adult book club groups as well.

Overall, the most important thing a librarian can do in a street-lit book club is to listen to the readers. For many teens, the library is one of a few places where they have the opportunity to really speak their minds about themselves and issues they face on a daily basis. The library street-lit book club can be an important platform where urban readers, specifically, can say how they relate to the stories (or not) in ways they need to say it; they also learn to listen to others as peers seek to voice their thoughts and be heard.

The teen library book club, when focusing on the genre of street lit, can be a forum for processing fictional and lived stories so that teens make meaning from living in communities that can be a fast-paced and unorganized atmosphere. The street-lit book club is a place where daily living can be slowed down and reflected on in slow motion, allowing opportunity for sense to be made out of nonsensical neighborhood happenings. Teens can validate their questions, insights, and fears while reconciling them for heightened self-understanding and determination.

Case in point, with the teens I worked with, when I began the book club, most of the book clubbers were in the sixth and seventh grades (circa 2005), with one or two attending high school at the time. Six years later, all of the middle schoolers are grown up and attending college and/or post-secondary trade school. Some of the older teens enlisted in the military with military tours in Iraq and Afghanistan. Some of the former library teens are parents now, working and living productive lives. The point here is that no one is in jail; no one is a prostitute or wifey, drug dealer or pimp from reading street lit or from being in a book club that focused on reading street lit. From observing the book clubbers' writings on Facebook, what I can attest to is that they all, at the time of this writing, are thinkers, readers, and writers. I cannot help but think that their involvement with their neighborhood library, library staff, and library activities, such as the street-lit book club, contributed to their reading lives today.

LIBRARIAN BOOK CLUBS

Library book club activities can help adults to center on self-reflection and inquiry that is geared toward personal and professional development. As part of my dissertation study, I worked with adult colleague librarians in a book club, reading street lit. We used the genre as a means of practitioner inquiry and professional development. Although with teens I focused on reading contemporary street lit, learning from the teens as they informed me of new authors, titles, songs, lyrics, artists—everything hip-hop—with the adults, we approached the genre from a historical perspective, reading titles along a literary continuum, such as writings by Stephen Crane, Paul Laurence Dunbar, Ann Petry, and Henry Roth, as discussed in chapter 2 of this book.

As a librarian book club, we also looked at various formats of library materials that featured stories about inner-city living, such as picture books (e.g., Ezra Jack Keats's *A Snowy Day* and *Goggles!*) and graphic novels (e.g., Donald Goines's *Daddy Cool*, 1974, which was reissued as a graphic novel; Eminem's biographical installment *In My Skin*, 2004).

Book club librarians learned strategies for readers' advisory for street lit (and genres across the board, for that matter) as well as for confronting ethical biases they didn't realize they were carrying toward patrons, the literature, and various professional practices, such as collection development and management. Various practitioner inquiry activities were introduced and employed (and were also successfully executed with the teen book clubbers):

Reaction Sheets

After intense book club discussions librarians wrote an anonymous paragraph or so recording their response to that session. The sheets were then collected by the facilitator. At the next book club meeting, the meeting opened up with the facilitator reading the responses. The responses then garnered further discussion. Reaction sheets were very useful for approaching hard-to-discuss topics.

Polling

We would often poll the group on questions that arose from the readings and discussion. For example, "How many of us have met Winter Santiaga [the protagonist of *The Coldest Winter Ever*] in the library? What was her information need? How did you meet that need?"

Word Associations

When prevalent themes took up a lot of the discussion's focus, we'd do a word association around a word or short phrase. Librarians would write down whatever words or phrases came to mind that they associated with the assigned meme. This stream-of-consciousness listing would last about one or two minutes. After the time was up, we shared our associations in round-robin fashion, which manifested matching ideas, new ideas, and opposing ideas. This outcome would lead to further discussion about personal beliefs and how they signify professional practice.

Check-In

At the beginning or at the end of the book club session, the facilitator would ask the group what is going on in their libraries: What is popular in your library right now? Who is checking out what? What are patrons saying about the collection? What do you think of that? Such questions open up space for participants to discuss and share professional experiences and best practices.

All of these methods are strategies for practitioner inquiry; invariably, these various group reflection activities brought up discussion about professional practice (Cochran-Smith and Lytle 2009). The very act of talking about the story, characters, and setting was enough for librarians to begin talking about their social interactions with patrons via readers' advisory and reference interviews. The majority of book club librarians report that practitioner inquiry helped them to perceive differently their ideas and understandings about their service community, definitions of reading, assumptions about street literature and its readers, and their overall stance toward their professional identity as librarians. Street literature was a catalyst for reflective professional development.

There are many inquiry exercises and activities that can be introduced to dig deeper into a book discussion to pull connections from the stories to contemplate personal and professional reading, writing, and literacy practices. Librarians (and other educators) filling the role as book club facilitators must provide a confidential space for discourse for both teen readers and adult readers of street lit. Because of various themes in the genre, such as violence, death, and sex, questions, connections, and experiences may be shared that require confidentiality. This doesn't mean that librarians and libraries become secret service counselors and agencies; it just means that everyone in the group respects one another's stories as sacred in the reading circle. This assurance serves as a foundation for authentic, open conversation and reflection pertaining to a genre that demands to be heard.

FIELD TRIPS

Author book signings and lectures are excellent field trips for street-lit book clubbers. Many street-lit authors like K'wan, Vickie Stringer, Teri Woods, and T. N. Baker visit schools, libraries, and other local outlets to meet readers and promote their books. As a field trip, a book club can visit a bookstore or another literary location that is hosting an author event. Movies are another type of field trip for a street-lit book club. Book festivals and fairs are other important venues where street-lit authors and panel discussions are featured. For example, the Harlem Book Fair in New York and the Philadelphia Free Library Book Festival feature authors and topics related to the street-literature genre.

Some field trips that have proved successful for programming for street lit include but are not limited to

- author book signings and events
- street lit in cinema (e.g., *Push* by Sapphire made into the movie *Precious*, 2009, or the recent film *Brooklyn's Finest*, 2010)
- book club meetings at a café instead of the library
- local university free lectures or events
- book fairs, festivals, and expos

- literacy outreach events, such as teens doing storytime at a day care, public and school librarians collaborating on an author visit, and teens distributing library program flyers at school
- cross-branch visits: for multibranch city library systems, you can network with other librarians and have your book club visit their book club, and vice versa

For managing teens on field trips, the best approach is to have them meet you at the venue. Urban teens are adept at independently navigating mass transportation in the city. Field trips to public events with teens are successful when the teacher or librarian consistently promotes the event and perhaps incentivizes attendance with a door prize or a prize presented at the next book club meeting. It is important that the teens understand that the event is free admission and that their attendance is their responsibility. Flyers can be posted in the library and also given to teens to share with their parents.

For the teen book club I facilitated, I promoted a street-lit author panel where I was the moderator for the event, at the Free Library of Philadelphia. I invited the book clubbers to the event, reminding them this was an opportunity for them to finally meet the authors they'd been reading so that they can ask questions. Of the fifteen book clubbers, six came to the event, sat up front, and asked Teri Woods a question during the Q&A portion of the program. This interaction led to Woods meeting and talking with the teens after the event, which further led to her personally visiting the book club at the library a month later. At the visit, she read over the book club's collaborative street-lit story outline and offered insightful feedback. This experience attests to how field trips for street lit can result in impactful outcomes.

PROMOTING STREET LIT = PROMOTING LITERACY

Small, rural, or suburban libraries may not have the demand for street lit like urban locales. Nevertheless, we do know that street lit is appealing to readers beyond urban locations and that every kind of reader is reading the genre. We know this to be true because quite a few street-lit titles have appeared on the New York Times Best-Seller List (e.g., *The Coldest Winter Ever*, *True to the Game*, *Thug Lovin'*, and *The Cartel—2*), which indicates that a broad spectrum of readers are buying and reading street lit. Case in point, Taylor Nix (2009, para. 3) of the Urban Book Source stated that "an appearance on the New York Times Best-Sellers List is proof that there is a place for America's inner-city tale that mirrors the realities and struggles of urban Black life on the street. [Street lit] is reaching audiences far beyond local community bookstores, exposing the masses to a new style of writing that has been overlooked and ignored by mainstream America until recently." This being said, it is a good idea for public library locations beyond the city to include a representation of street-lit titles on library shelves. This representation would be best based on appropriate age and reading levels (teen-friendly versus A/YA street lit), as well as patron interest.

We can see how library programming that is focused on or related to street lit may engage library patrons to check out more books and participate in library activities. However, enough cannot be said for the presence of the librarian as a promoter and supporter of street lit as an entry into the act of reading, in and of itself. Street lit can serve as a gateway to a broader reading regimen; indeed, I have worked with street kids whose first fully read book (from cover to cover) was a street-lit title. Their sense of accomplishment at successfully reading a book motivated them to read another book, then another book, then another. I am proud to share that, as of this writing, those teens are now attending college.

Once I did a poll of the teen book clubbers in the North Philadelphia library I worked at and later volunteered at, and asked them, "What books have you read in the past six months?" It was Christmas season at that time, so that meant they were recalling titles read from the end of the previous school year (June) to the end of the calendar year (December). Of the fifteen teens (eleven girls and four boys) who were there that day, we filled the blackboard with more than 50 different titles (not including multiple references to the Harry Potter series), spanning eight distinct genres: mystery, romance, science fiction, African American biographies, classics, fantasy, horror, and poetry.

As illustrated in this chapter, reading street lit can be a powerful means to introduce and immerse readers into an exploration of reading a broad range of text. It is a worthy approach to push or promote street lit because it has been shown that it does engage even the reluctant or nontraditional reader in other kinds of literacy activities, such as more varied reading of literary genres, writing various forms of prose, and creative artistic self-expression. Reading street lit but also talking about and around street lit can spawn an exploration of reading the self—the self as a reader, the self as a writer, the self as an artist, the self as a literate being in multiple contexts. I do not know any educator who would find a problem with that.

EPILOGUE

BEEF: Bringin' Extreme Explanations
to the Forefront of Street Lit

What follows is a spirited email dialogue between myself when I was a columnist for *Library Journal* (at the time of this email exchange) and author-educator Zetta Elliott, whose young adult novel *A Wish after Midnight* was published in 2010 to favorable reviews. Our paths crossed in December 2009 when I came across Elliott's novel while searching for prepublication works for *Library Journal*'s "Word on the Street Lit" column.

After reading the blurb for *Wish*, I requested an advance copy of the novel to determine whether it was appropriate for the street-lit column. Upon receipt of the galley, I received an email from Elliott seeking clarity on how *Wish* would be situated in the column. From this initial exchange, I decided to withdraw the review. However, we continued our email conversation over the course of a week, debating the pros and cons of street lit, which raised important positions and ideas from both sides of the street-lit debate. This dialogue became a candid conversation in which Elliott and I shared our views on the merits and limitations of street lit to further understand the value of literature alongside the value of the reader, especially in the realm of public librarianship. The dialogue occurred from December 9 to December 13, 2009, and is detailed here in chronological order, with permission.

From: "Morris, Vanessa"
To: Zetta Elliott
Sent: Wednesday, December 9, 2009 11:25:54 PM
Subject: RE: Wish

Hi Zetta;

Thanks for emailing me. I love your book—point blank. And I intend to review it for the "Word on the Street Lit" column, with a full introduction presenting a discussion about Street Literature being more than just novels about the rawness and grittiness of inner city living, but also, elucidating the fact that the genre is about the diverse experiences of a diverse population that live in inner city communities. Everyday experiences include the mundane AND the fantastical—everywhere—and that "everywhere" includes the hood.

Earlier this week, your publisher sent an email requesting that your novel not be reviewed for the column—that "Street Literature" is the wrong categorization for the book. My editor emailed me to ask me my thoughts on the matter. Here is my response:

"I am reading this cute little book right now, and it is YA lit, OK. But it is also a nice twist on Street Lit, in the sense that it is a story about a young girl living in inner city Brooklyn, amid hardships and the usual characters in the hood, but she circumvents the negatives of the street, and has an adventure that goes into the realm of fantasy and sci fi, since time travel is involved. This can be considered also, speculative fiction—a branch of fantasy/sci fi that includes stories about urban experiences—there are speculative fiction titles that I would also cross reference into Street Lit, namely Nalo Hopkinson's Brown Girl in the Ring *(1998), L.A. Banks'* Minion *(2003) and even Octavia Butler's* Mind of My Mind *(1977). It is about defining Street Literature as being location and space-specific—the street as a character that influences other characters' choices and behaviors, the street as a stage upon which various stories are enacted.*

I don't think I appreciate the publisher's request, in the sense that—if I hadn't found the dangit book, we wouldn't even be reviewing it—so now they want to tell us how to categorize it? Interesting.

Anyhoo, the fact that this IS a twist on Street Lit is precisely why I am excited to read and review it for the column. This goes right into our recent discussions about turning the page on how we are defining contemporary Street Literature— supporting the genre as a broadstroke of varied city experiences from various cultural locations (Genna, the protagonist in this book, is Panamanian and African American). More importantly, Genna tells truths about inner city living that are thoughtful and important to add to the discourse surrounding Street Lit.

Perhaps we can tell the publisher that we will review it as a YA novel, indeed—but on the Street Lit column—to encourage educators and readers to broaden their understanding and concept of what Street Literature actually is, and what stories it offers to readers everywhere. I can provide a nice introduction addressing this as the focus for the month—thereby also highlighting any elements of the other books reviewed that also expands the definition of Street Lit. In fact, if they agree, right now—this book is my pick for the month.

As you know I am running two librarian Street Lit book clubs for my dissertation study. For this month—we are reading picture books. Just wanted to share that, to illustrate how far reaching Street Lit can be as a genre, just like romance, historical fiction, mystery, biography, etc.

Whaddayathink? I hope they don't fight us on this. This little gem of a novel has the potential to contribute to the turn of the tide that is happening with heightening the literary value of contemporary Street Literature.

Vanessa."

Zetta, I hope my sharing this with you helps to clarify my intention for reviewing your wonderful novel. And I sincerely hope that it is OK—with you.

Sincerely,
Vanessa Morris

From: Zetta Elliott
Sent: Thursday, December 10, 2009 12:04 AM
To: Morris,Vanessa
Subject: Re: Wish

THIS is why I wanted to do an interview to accompany your review . . . and I *prayed* that it WAS you doing the review (nothing against your co-columnist) . . . I really liked what you had to say in your Writers against Racism interview, and AJM [AJM is a mutual librarian friend of Vanessa and Zetta] said that you had been introducing different YA books into your Street Lit column . . . but let me just be honest: it was NOT my publisher who fought the review, it was ME. Once I heard Marketing was sending *LJ* a review copy of *Wish,* I let them know that I was VERY concerned.

I don't write "Street Lit." The teachers [I know] don't endorse "Street Lit" or . . . use it in the classroom. "Street Lit" doesn't get considered for a Coretta Scott King Award. I felt that linking my novel (which is literary fiction) with the genre commonly referred to as "Street Lit" was a huge tactical error, and I told my publisher that I found it deeply offensive. I signed with them because I believed they were doing something radically different than the traditional publishing industry—which has all but STOPPED publishing black literary fiction in favor of books that are poorly written and only glamorize aspects of urban life commonly referred to as "ghetto." I also pointed them to the description given by one of the reviewers for the "Street Lit" column:

"Typical elements include a rags-to-riches theme, references to the hip-hop music industry, profanity, urban slang, erotic sex scenes, criminal activity, or violence that escalates to murder. But that's just part of it. Often the story line is circular so that plot points from the novel's opening pages come into play at the climax."

My publisher didn't seek out this column, but I just wanted to make sure that as they developed promotional strategies for *Wish*, they considered the consequences of having my novel linked with titles like *Something on the Side*, *Down Low Sistahs*, and *Still Hood*.

So it was me who balked—not at the general idea of a review in your column, but in your review being the FIRST for *Wish* . . . I may just be an elitist snob, but to me there's a HUGE difference between Street Lit and what I would call urban narratives—and that's partly what *my* dissertation was on! I'd love to talk with you more about your project of reframing the Street Lit genre . . . I can't say I'd be in favor of that, but then I haven't read much Street Lit and can't speak to its possible connections with the urban narratives I've studied (for example, *Push* isn't Street Lit to me, but *The Coldest Winter Ever* is . . . and it didn't make it into my thesis for that reason). I honestly think of *Wish* as the antithesis—and possibly the antidote!—to Street Lit. I respect the right of authors to write whatever they like, and there's clearly demand for these kinds of stories. But to place those books next to the novels of James Baldwin simply because they all take place in the city? It's a stretch . . . for me, at least.

So let me know if there's anything I can do to contribute to the discussion . . . and I sincerely hope my views haven't offended you. I really do appreciate that you're trying to help librarians read these novels in a way that helps them to connect with a particular audience and a larger literary tradition. And I'd love for readers of *Hood Rat* to pick up *A Wish after Midnight*. But I wouldn't embrace the term Street Lit or use it to describe what I do. I'll be interested to see how you connect *Wish* to the other books you've read . . . and if we can't do an interview for *LJ*, maybe you'd agree to do an interview for my blog?

Z

From: "Morris,Vanessa"
To: Zetta Elliott
Sent: Thursday, December 10, 2009 1:25:40 AM
Subject: RE: Wish

Zetta,

I didn't know anything about your request to do an interview with the review.

Respectful of your concerns, I will pass on reviewing *Wish* for the column. I do not have the power to suggest that *LJ* do anything else with the book, but your publisher might want to send another galley to the Young Adult department for *LJ*. Trustfully, they will consider it.

Your stance on Street Lit sitting alongside canonical literature speaks to the same issues we have as a people. For example, when thinking about issues of class, wealthy citizens tend to be socio-economically at odds with lower income citizens and vice versa. My position though, is that everyone's story is classic, because, it is LIVED. I wonder if James Baldwin and other black authors of yesteryear would raise an eyebrow to your statement because while they all may not have agreed on what each other may have written, I don't believe they ever belabored anyone's right to write, to express, to publish what they believed to be their story to tell. Even black authors who disagreed about the literary, social and/or cultural merits of one another's work (i.e., James Baldwin/Richard Wright and Langston Hughes/Zora Neale Hurston) ultimately became neighbors on library bookshelves, sitting side-by-side . . . on the shelf—canonical. The same will happen with Sister Souljah and Edward P. Jones. History tells us so.

I'm glad we've connected.

Best wishes, Vanessa Morris

From: Zetta Elliott
Sent: Thursday, December 10, 2009 8:46 AM
To: Morris,Vanessa
Subject: Re: Wish

Oh dear . . . so I take it the idea of you doing the review for *LJ*, and me doing an interview for my blog doesn't appeal to you? This is a debate I'd really like to have in public so that more voices can chime in. I do realize my position seems elitist, but I still think there are important distinctions to be made between content and form, narrative intent, and ultimately—quality. Hurston was criticized by some for writing *about* the folk and for using "dialect" . . . in large part because the dominant white culture already favored certain "types" of African Americans and would fasten onto such representations as "authentic," dismissing the writing on black middle class people or even elites. Richard Wright was Hurston's nemesis, was celebrated by whites, and yet ultimately did the exact same thing with Bigger—"the black beast/brute." Their public exchange was really productive, but ultimately both were literary writers. And James Baldwin ultimately came out with a harsh critique of *Native Son* as a deeply flawed novel. Black people aren't monolithic; we definitely want books that represent the full range of our values and experiences. But that doesn't mean we don't self-select as well . . .

At any rate, I could go on and on. Maybe one day we'll get a chance to discuss this on a conference panel or something. I do apologize if I gave offense by sharing my reservations.

Zetta

From: "Morris,Vanessa"
To: Zetta Elliott
Sent: Thursday, December 10, 2009 5:20:05 PM
Subject: RE: Wish

With the review for *LJ*—the interview would be cursory, at best, due to spacing requirements for the column. I recently did an interview with Teri Woods, and it was whittled down. So—I do not think that is the best space for an in-depth, thoughtful and passionate interview that our conversation would undoubtedly represent.

Me doing an interview for your blog? I'd be honored. Yes, I'd like that . . .
As to being offended—well yeah. lol. But like I said earlier, this isn't necessarily a bad thing. It's a good thing—being offended means there's unpacking to be done. And for this, I am most grateful to you for our conversation. I'd rather us communicate and help each other in our thinking than to just do a review and it be all complicated.

I'm offended for layered reasons—most of them personal—in the sense that I come from the ghetto—and I know the stories, as spelled out in Street Lit—to be authentically real. Do some people live with that much conflict, and perhaps confusion, day after day? Yes. Do some people talk with slang as their primary vernacular? Yes. Do some people treat each other with distrust and betrayal (like all humans can do)? Yes. Are people in the hood sexual and at times violent (like all humans are)? Um—yeah.

But also—the genre shows inner city communities as just that—communities. So you do have Street Lit that shows diverse neighborhoods with not just characters of African descent, but also Asian, Latino, and Whites. A lot of Street Lit is a dictation of how upper, middle, and lower class experiences intersect and overlap: stories about drug dealers becoming rich, but not understanding their wealth, and thereby squandering it, redemption stories of young people growing up and having to still clean up past loose ends, relationships between women and men and how lost we feel (on both sides) in trying to make sense of what love feels like, looks like, acts like. Elders characterized as the moral compasses by which the protagonists and antagonists measure themselves or are measured. I think more importantly what grabs me about Street Lit is that is dares to tell the stories of our wounds as a diverse group of people—those stories that usually get shoved under the rug because they are so ugly, so fantastical, so unbelievable, yet they are real, they have happened to real people. Truth be told, a lot of the stories are set in the 1980's and this is no accident. The black community had a community fallout during that time, with the crack epidemic and the "drug war" both very active. Today's Street Lit historicizes that time in ways that many social commentary texts do not and . . . cannot.

Recently I was talking to a friend of mine and she was telling me about how at her law office everyone was passing around *Push* by Sapphire. She said to me, "Can you believe that that's a real story? A biography?" I had to correct her. We got into a thing about it, because she was *convinced* that the story was real. Of course it is real in the sense that it is based on real experiences of students Sapphire worked with during her time as a literacy instructor in Harlem . . . but it's intent and packaging is fiction. I believe that with Street Literature there IS a gray line between the real and the fictive, non-fiction and fiction. Elijah Anderson's works (for example) can be set beside say, Jihad's *Street Life* or Antonne M. Jones's *The Family* and there are similarities in characters, setting, and experiences. Yet one is non-fiction, the others are fiction. What point does it make to say that Anderson's non-fiction work is better than the others? Or that it is "quality?" As a librarian, "quality" literature for me is—the literature that inspires and motivates a human being to READ. Because once a person acquires the habit for reading, things can only go up from there.

This is the value that Street Lit brings to the people who read the genre. My adopted daughter, as well as other teens I've worked with over the years, has proudly stated, "The first book I ever read from cover to cover was *True to the Game* (or *Coldest Winter Ever* or *Flyy Girl*)." That statement has been said to me many times. Also, just because people read Street Literature doesn't mean that that is the only thing they read. I did a poll in December of 2007 with a group of about 15 North Philadelphia teens and they reported over 50 titles and 7 genres between them that they read within a six-month period.

My librarian bookclub just read (or re-read) Wright's *Native Son* this past October. What makes you think it is not Street Literature? Everything that happens in that book—happens on the street. And I do not see Bigger as a black beast or brute. He is not just a character in a novel; he is representative of the human condition, *a human being*—oft times wounded, flawed, frustrated, unhappy, confused. (Have you read Wright's essay, "How Bigger Was Born?") In that essay he talks about how his inspiration for telling Bigger's story came out of his observations of the rage of poor men from EUROPE and RUSSIA. He wanted to let the world know that black people are angry too. The librarians at the bookclub session were like, "It shocks me that it is 70 years after the publication of this book, and the story is still familiar—still true today." And pointedly, Cornel West has intimated in various interviews and in his writings, that 'black rage' at the inequalities and injustices of a patriarchal, hegemonic society, like America is alive and well today. Come on now.

And truth be told, I adopted a Precious. My adopted daughter is now a college student. But when I met her 10 years ago, she was a quiet, shy 8 year-old foster kid who had been sodomized by her stepfather. So yeah—in the movie, just make Precious an eight-year-old little girl—and you got a very real, live, breathing Precious. So for me? Precious' story is not just real—it's a thick seam in the tapestry of my life. And for me, her story is very street. Perpetrators do what they do as outcomes of living street lives. People who are living unpredictable days (like foster children often do) are all too frequently victims of such perpetrators. And then, the streets themselves serve as a thruway for people and their experiences. For example, in the movie, "Precious," it is the street that escorts Precious from home to school to the hospital to the social worker and back home again. In inner city communities, the streets are powerful navigational channels through which lives are not just lived, but often negotiated, and re-negotiated again. There is a different way of being when you come from the hood. And the Street Lit genre—as it is articulated today—is telling some important stories that we need to listen to, about what it is like living in low-income city communities in the 21st century. In my life, it was the street that brought me to the library as a pre-teen, teen, and then adult patron, and ultimately as a public librarian in the hood. It was the street that brought my daughter to me. And it was Street Lit that made her a reader, and therefore played a signifying role in why she is in college, at this very moment, as I write this email to you.

Back in 1893, Stephen Crane went through the same struggle to get his first novel told (*Maggie, A Girl of the Streets*), as Street Lit authors attest to today. He self published his first novel (just like Teri Woods and many others have done in current times) because publishers thought the book was too sexy, too raw, too violent, and poorly written because of the dialect (Irish ghetto slang). After *The Red Badge of Courage* became a bestseller, publishers revisited and sanitized *Maggie, A Girl of the Streets,* before mainstream publishing it. It is now considered a feminist canonical text today. That's just one example of a ghetto story outliving its historical context—there are plenty.

You mentioned that we, as cultural community, self-select our reads. So true. This includes African Americans (or otherwise) who read Street Literature. I can tell you stories about how teens and adults would come into the library and would know the title, author, and publisher of the books they wanted to read. I would be working with them to pick out a book, and they were very clear about what they wanted to read—even in the realm of Street Lit. Have you been down to 125th Street in Harlem, say, in the past year or so? The books are changing. Street Lit stories are starting to be more about "What happens after I stop dealing or hooking?" "How do I pull myself up and out of this ghetto?" "How does the family and the community heal from violence and lack of resources?" The genre is doing what genres do—it is maturing. Street Lit is maturing to the point where the cream rises to the top and the rest, well—they don't make money, and they stop being published, and you start to get a standard for the genre.

Lastly, I'll leave you with my latest Facebook status from last night—around 1:00 A.M.:

"Jeff Toobin, on CNN, just described the life timeline of one of the U.S. young men arrested for possible terrorism in Pakistan (divorced parents, a lot of moving, drug informant for FBI, yadda). After he finished, he said, "Did you get all that? Can you believe it? It's like a novel."

I look forward to hearing from you.

Sincerely,
Vanessa

From: Zetta Elliott
Sent: Thursday, December 10, 2009 9:02 PM
To: Morris,Vanessa
Subject: Re: Wish

Great—I'll start compiling some questions for our interview. Is before Xmas too hectic for you? I'll send the questions once they're ready, and you can get them back to me whenever you have a chance.

There's a sort of anti-Street Lit campaign out there—do you know about it? Or rather, it's a pro-literary fiction movement . . . two authors are spearheading it: Donna Grant and Virginia DeBerry, I think? Carleen Brice has also tackled the issue at her blog, White Readers Meet Black Authors. I could respond to a few topics, but honestly am not qualified to discuss Street Lit in depth because I haven't read that much of it . . . if you felt there was one particular title we could all respond to, maybe we could do analyses of that novel and one we agree is urban/literary?

My review of *Tyrell* gets a lot of hits—still—and I wrote it quite a while ago. The second link tackles the definition of "ghetto" and that's a topic I'd like to revisit:

http://zettaelliott.wordpress.com/2009/07/20/a-tangled-web/

http://zettaelliott.wordpress.com/2009/08/02/keepin-it-real/

I can more easily respond to YA lit than to adult lit these days, but we can save that conversation for the interview on my blog. I have NO problem with novels trying to represent the realities of ALL black people. Really. That is not my problem with Street Lit (the little I've read, and what I've heard about the genre in general). My issue is with the quality of the writing itself. I haven't seen *Precious*, but I do teach *Push* and though I felt the novel lacked restraint (bad editing, not bad writing) I judge it as a whole—WHAT it's saying, and HOW it's making its points. There is certainly a kind of snobbery and prudishness that dismisses Street Lit as just so much smut; the same people can't stand rap music and want to ban 50 Cent. I'm not part of that crowd. I'm not trying to censor anyone. But I'm not going to call something "great literature" simply because it holds a mirror up to reality. That's not what art does—it shows what's real AND what's possible. So if you're seeing progress in the genre, and stories about "uplift" and ambition, that's great. And I can definitely see a scholarly project that tracks reader response and the ways readers (of various classes) negotiate these texts, and extract or generate meaning from the narratives. I do think readers can love Toni Morrison and find Street Lit compelling. Different texts, different reading experiences. But there's no WAY a complex novel like *Jazz* (which I would call an urban narrative) belongs next to Street Lit; the complexity, the nuance, the historical references, the literary devices—all of that elevates the book in terms of literary merit (for me). I'll have to take your word for it if you say Street Lit novels share that complexity. If you put rich, middle class, and working class black people in a room, they wouldn't all smile and get along just because they're black. We differentiate ourselves based on gender, age, religion, sexual orientation, region, class, profession, etc. And because we're all hybrid, many of our identities overlap. I'm OK with that. But we don't try to erase those differences—they define who we are. I think literature should be classified according to certain criteria—just like your co-columnist reviewer defined Street Lit in that first column. It's worthwhile to read texts against one another to look for similarities and differences, but we don't have to conclude that they're the same. What's valuable to me may not be valuable to another reader. And that's ok . . . have you read *Erasure* by Percival Everett? a *brilliant* satire of *Native Son,* Street Lit, and pretentious literary/academic writers . . .

OK, I'm going to draft a few questions. I guess I'll frame it as a conversation that arose from your interest in *Wish* . . . or I could leave that out and just talk about realism in urban YA lit . . .

Zetta Elliott

From: "Morris,Vanessa"
To: Zetta Elliott
Sent: Thursday, December 11, 2009 4:29:07 PM
Subject: RE: Wish

Hey Zetta!

Truthfully, I'd rather do the questions after the holiday, when life is a bit more sane for me. I promise it will get done by the end of this month, for sure.

I wanted to respond to your email:

You said: "My issue is with the quality of the writing itself. I haven't seen Precious, but I do teach Push and though I felt the novel lacked restraint (bad editing, not bad writing) I judge it as a whole—WHAT it's saying, and HOW it's making its points.

Here's my thing: does literature always have to make a point? Or rather, isn't there are "point" in literature NOT making a point sometimes? Or is it about the fact that each reader gets a different point out of what he/she deems as literature? S.R. Ranganathan (1892–1972) is a founding father of library science. He elucidated the "5 laws of Library Science" as thus:

1. Books are for use.
2. Every book its reader.
3. Every reader his (her) book.
4. Save the time of the reader.
5. The library is a growing organism.

So for me, as a librarian, it is the reader who decides what literature is and what it is not. I have noticed that what happens in a patriarchal, capitalistic society, like the U.S., is that it is mainstream America that "decides" what "quality" is and what is "literature" for everyone, which includes citizens who exist on the margins. What then happens is that those who are marginalized, when seeking voice for their own stories, are cowed by the mainstream to conform their sense of what is, and what is not, to the definitions that the mainstream has already determined. In the library, on the front lines, democracy rears its head and challenges this hegemony all the time. So you have patrons who will be like: "I want to read this. We want this in our library." It is the librarian who is the liaison between the mainstream and the fringed who offers up traditional, *mainstream* literary values, but also creates and maintains equal space for *localized,* non-traditional literary values (this is one aspect of the concept, "equitable access" in librarianship). Between the *2 realms*, new space is created to add new texts to the literary shelf. This tension between the mainstream and the localized is how new authors become literary or canonical, actually. It's the souping up of the local, to the global, and situating it in the mainstream. This is what Street Lit is doing. This is what all genres *do*. It is a natural course of literature as an organic art form, it is the solar system after the big bang, the adult that emerges from childhood. All genres go through a maturation process, and then they sit—collect and standardize themselves—then get resurrected, renaissanced, and morphed into another level (which is also what current Street Lit is doing—think Donald Goines and Iceberg Slim of the 1970s).

You also talked about how "[t]here is certainly a kind of snobbery and prudishness that dismisses Street Lit as just so much smut; the same people can't stand rap music and want to ban 50 Cent. I'm not part of that crowd. I'm not trying to censor anyone. But I'm not going to call something "great literature" simply because it holds a mirror up to reality. That's not what art does—it shows what's real AND what's possible."

All in all, I think art does different things for different people—and that's the beauty of it. What I get out of Frida Kahlo, Susan Sontag or Frank Morrison (my favorite artists) is going to be totally different than what anyone else gets out of it—including the artist her/himself. I do agree that there is a common "group consciousness" if you will, that surrounds art, to determine if it *is what it says it is* and that is-ness is part of a larger conversation, meaning—whether there is local appeal to the art or global appeal to art. Art gains voice by a collective acknowledgement of what it is, and what it is not. I don't think it has anything to do with whether it's uplifting or demeaning. I think art messes with consciousness because—it does—that's what it do.

In terms of the genre progressing and now including stories about uplift and ambition, Street Lit is doing what genres do—it is simmering down—settling in— *finding its place on the proverbial collective cultural shelf.* However, I don't think it's because it's now saying better things, I think it is because it is now saying things *better;* which is part of that organic process I'm talking about. It's like you babble before you become fluent in the language. Street Lit's been babbling for a few years, and now it's starting to speak fluently. So like, even the pioneers can't come out with that same shit they used to drop a few years back. For example, I recently gave a less than stellar review on a Relentless Aaron title because it was not his usual high standard. Readers are looking for more—for *better*—and thus, the genre is maturing. (Every book its reader/Every reader his/her book.)

The way I see it—each book has its own complexity and nuance, and that is solely up to the reader.

Zetta, I continue to think about how Street Lit is defined. Please know that I have problems with the definition of Street Lit as projected via the early days of the *LJ* column. That definition was offered up two years ago when the column was brand new and wasn't particularly based from a framework of situating and *respecting* the genre as part of a literary continuum and tradition that has a history and perhaps even a social legacy.

I agree with you that it's worthwhile to read texts against one another to look for similarities and differences, but we don't have to conclude that they're the same.

Coincidentally, your mention of *Erasure* by Percival Everett is synchronistic because the librarian bookclubs are reading it for January. I'll keep you posted as to what the responses are—I anticipate they will be fascinating. Straight up—it's going to blow their minds.

You said there is an anti-Street Lit movement going on. This is hilarious to me. I think of the brothers and sisters in the hood, pushing their carts to the stores, pounding the pavement from job to job, in the beauty salons, barbershops, restaurants, *and drug rehabs*, hangin' on the corners, stoops, and porches, smokin' their As, drinkin' their 40s, ridin' the subways and Els while *reading Street Lit*, going into libraries and night classes trying to learn how to use computers, attending class at community colleges and trade schools, raisin' children, readin,' feedin,' and bein' with their children . . . and don't get me started about the daily lives of our kin in prison *who read and write Street Lit* . . . and the best that our "contemporary authors" can do is wage a campaign against their own cultural kin's stories? HILARIOUS. How about they just write stories that people will want to read? How 'bout that? How 'bout they go up in the hood and learn those stories and write those stories *their* way (like you did, Zetta). Again—every book its reader—every reader his/her book. Ah well. Gotta love it.

From: Zetta Elliott
Sent: Friday, December 11, 2009 9:48 PM
To: Morris,Vanessa
Subject: Re: Wish

Hey, Vanessa. I *finally* figured out why we've been missing each other . . . I've shared parts of your emails with two of my literary scholar friends, and they've questioned some of your terms. But your last email clarifies a LOT—I told one friend you seemed more like a sociologist and I realize now that you *are* a social scientist—library science is totally new to me, and I think it's connected to literary studies but is also quite distinct. When you say two very different books will be on the same shelf, I think of the literary canon as it is taught in universities. Which is different than what's made available in a bookstore or public library . . . I get it! And I absolutely feel that ALL literary options should be available in public libraries—a book for every reader—definitely. But as a professor of literature, I'm doing something slightly different because I'm training my students the same way I was trained; I introduce texts I find problematic not because I think they're "worthy," but because they can teach students something . . . I don't really admire Tyler Perry as a filmmaker, but he's on the film course syllabus because reading his film against another trains the students' critical eye. I see my job as introducing students to books they might not find on their own, but also giving them critical skills to read, analyze, and critique the book, helping them to situate the book in relation to other texts produced within a culture, and showing them how to use themes or structures in the book to theorize their own experience. With library science, there's actually a lot more trust placed in the reader . . . use the book for whatever purpose you like—there's less mediation and/or interference in the reading process itself, and yet as great mediation in the SELECTION process . . . you have more power, in a way, because as I explained to the Bronx students I talked to today, I couldn't afford to buy books as a child. I still only buy books as gifts for others; for myself, I rely almost entirely upon the public library system. Their teacher bought 45 copies of *Wish* for four classes, and the kids loved it so much they STOLE the books to take home and read ahead. She now has 11 copies, which means there won't be enough books to teach next year's classes. And to me, that's unbearable because *I* was the kid who depended on books being available in school and at the library. And when I was their age, there were almost NO black books in my public library. So you're right—it's incredibly damaging if the library selection committee thinks they know what's best for the ENTIRE reading population.

Public libraries ought to serve the masses, so I appreciate that the *LJ* column introduces librarians to the value and meaning and legitimacy of Street Lit.

. . . A big part of [other Black authors'] critique, however, is not with the actual quality of Street Lit—it's that mainstream publishers now only acquire books that will sell as well as Street Lit sells . . . and editors apply pressure, asking black writers to add hotter sex scenes, more violence, etc., because THOSE gatekeepers really don't give a damn about literary merit or pleasing a wide audience of readers . . . they only see dollar signs. Bernice McFadden talks about "seg-book-gation" . . . she doesn't want her book to be put in the "black" section of the bookstore because that limits its audience (and suggests that black readers share the same taste in books, and read according to an author's race rather than by genre) . . . As a self-published author, I know what she's talking about . . . five years of presses rejecting my novel with no valid reason; no complaints about the quality of the writing, just a feeling it wouldn't sell. So the proliferation of Street Lit also speaks to the lack of power blacks have as gatekeepers in publishing . . . [some] whites have an insatiable appetite for black pathology, and will exclude all other stories in favor of the ones that make them feel justified in having most of the power in this society . . .

OK, I better eat something or this headache will blossom. Post-holidays is absolutely fine for the interview . . .

nite

z

From: "Morris,Vanessa"
To: Zetta Elliott
Sent: Sunday, December 13, 2009 1:21:52 PM
Subject: RE: Wish

Hey Zetta;

I just want to let you know that I am not neglecting our conversation—just bogged down with grading papers. So as soon as I am lifted from closing out the Fall term, I will most definitely write you back, in full.

In the meantime though, I've shared our dialogue with the bookclub librarians.

The Philadelphia librarians will be discussing it today—they can't wait!—and the Westchester, NY, librarians are extending an invitation to have you come to their January meeting (January 29th), to join our discussion of Percival Everett's novel, *Erasure.*

This is all preliminary feedback, again will write more in full later—to further talk about, how while what I've stated is how librarians are to respond to community tastes for literature, that the issue with Street Lit, and anything else that librarians (and teachers) deem "not worthy" HAS been censored . . . librarians can be the most egregious of censors sometimes—this is an ongoing topic in library science graduate school classrooms.

■ ■ ■ ■ ■

Zetta Elliott accepted the Westchester Librarians' Book Club invitation and attended their January librarians' book club meeting to discuss Percival Everett's novel *Erasure*. Elliott also donated galley copies of her novel *A Wish after Midnight* to the librarian book clubs in Westchester and Philadelphia. Vanessa Morris submitted an interview to Elliott's blog and broadcast a video interview via Elliott's YouTube channel. Morris and Elliott have become friends and continue to keep in touch.

To read Morris's blog interview with Zetta Elliott, see

http://zettaelliott.wordpress.com/2010/01/25/what-is-street-lit/.

To view Elliott's video interview with Morris, see

http://www.youtube.com/watch?v=5BDqeWFIiJo.

Zetta Elliott's blog, *Fledgling,* lives at

http://zettaelliott.wordpress.com.

Vanessa Irvin Morris's blog, *Street Literature,* lives at

http://streetliterature.blogspot.com.

APPENDIX

Street-Literature Publishers

Akashic Books
www.akashicbooks.com
The Armory imprint: Kenji Jasper, "D"

Augustus Publishing
www.augustuspublishing.com
Authors: Shannon Holmes, Anthony Whyte, Erick S. Gray

Black Dawn Books (Publisher: K'wan)
http://blackdawnbooks.net
Authors: Sonny Black, Terry Wroten

The Cartel Publications
http://thecartelpublications.com
Authors: T. Styles, Reign

DC Bookdiva
www.dcbookdiva.com
Author: Dutch

Déjà Vu Publications
www.dejavupublications.com
Author: Deborah Cardona

Flowers in Bloom Publishing
www.flowersinbloompublishing.com
Author: J. M. Benjamin

Note: Authors often move from publisher to publisher. This list is not exhaustive.

GhettoHeat Publishing
http://ghettoheat.com
Authors: Jason Poole, Damon Meadows

Gorilla Convict Publications
www.gorillaconvict.com
Author: Seth Ferranti

Grand Central Publishing
Hachette Book Group
www.hachettebookgroup.com
Authors: Teri Woods, Wahida Clark, Kia Dupree, Jeff Rivera

Harlem Book Center
www.harlembookcenter.com
Authors: Sidi, Asante Kahari

Harlequin—eHarlequin.com
www.eharlequin.com/store.html?cid=590
Kimani Tru imprint, Kimani Tru series

Kensington Publishing Corp.
www.kensingtonbooks.com
Dafina imprint: Kiki Swinson, Drama High series, Daiimah S. Poole, Ni-Ni Simone
Holloway House imprint: Donald Goines, Iceberg Slim
Vibe Street Lit imprint: Kenji Jasper

Melodrama Publishing, LLC
Melodrama Publishing
www.melodramapublishing.com
Authors: Kiki Swinson, Endy

Norcarjo Publishing
www.norcarjo.com
Author: Dwayne Vernon

North Atlantic Books
www.northatlanticbooks.com/store/frog_feat/
Frog LTD imprint: Renay Jackson

Penguin Group USA (Viking Juvenile)

http://us.penguingroup.com/static/pages/publishers/adult/viking
.html
Author: Paul Volponi

Precioustymes Entertainment

www.precioustymes.com/homeNew.htm
*Authors: Platinum Teen series, KaShamba Williams, Chunichi, Noire, Nikki
Turner*

Random House

http://one-world.atrandom.com
One World/Ballantine imprint: Nikki Turner, Risque
Harlem Mood imprint: Clarence Nero

RJ Publications

http://rjpublications.com
Authors: Richard Jeanty, Shawn Black

St. Martin's Press

http://us.macmillan.com/SMP.aspx
*St. Martin's Griffin imprint: Tracy Brown, K'wan Foye, Shannon Holmes,
Relentless Aaron*
St. Martin's Paperbacks imprint: Mia Edwards

Simon and Schuster

www.simonandschuster.com
Author: Omar Tyree
Atria imprint: Sister Souljah, Snoop Dogg
G-Unit imprint: 50 Cent
Simon Pulse imprint: Todd Strasser, Allison van Diepen

Strebor Books (Publisher: Zane)

http://store.zanestore.com/street.html
Strebor on the Streets imprint: Caleb Alexander, Reginald L. Hall

Teri Woods Publishing

http://teriwoodspublishing.com/site.html
Authors: Teri Woods, Kwame Teague

Townsend Press
www.townsendpress.com/product/97.aspx
Authors: Bluford High series, Paul Langan, Anne Schraff

Triple Crown Publications
www.triplecrownpublications.com
Authors: Vickie Stringer, Will Robbins, Tu-Shonda Whitaker, Deja King, Keisha Ervin

Urban Books/Q-Boro Books
www.urbanbooks.net
Authors: T. N. Baker, Terra Little, Denim Diaries series, Ashley and JaQuavis, Chunichi, JaQuavis Coleman, Ashley Antoinette, Keisha Ervin, Laurinda D. Brown

W. W. Norton (Old School Books)
http://books.wwnorton.com/books/book-template.aspx?ser=Old +School+Books&currentpage=1&lastpage=4
Old School imprint: Clarence Cooper Jr., Chester Himes, Roland S. Jefferson, Iceberg Slim, Donald Goines

Wahida Clark Presents Publishing
www.wahidaclarkpublishing.com
Authors: Victor L. Martin, Mike Sanders, Missy Jackson, Cash, Tasha Hawthorne

STREET LIT AUTHOR WEB CONNECTIONS

This is a brief, nonexhaustive listing of the websites for the most salient contemporary authors.

Black Artemis: www.blackartemis.com

Tracy Brown: http://us.macmillan.com/author/tracybrown

Chunichi: www.myspace.com/chunichiwrites

Wahida Clark: http://wclarkpublishing.com/

De'nesha Diamond: http://deneshadiamond.com/

L. Divine: www.dramahigh.com

J. Love: http://jlovebooks.com/index.html

Ashley and JaQuavis: www.ashleyjaquavis.com

K'wan: http:// kwanfoye.com

Joy Deja King: http://joykingonline.com

Meesha Mink: www.meeshamink.com

Ni Ni Simone: www.myspace.com/nini_simone

Sister Souljah: http://sistersouljah.com

Vickie Stringer: www.triplecrownpublications.com

Kiki Swinson: www.kikiswinson.net

Nikki Turner: www.nikkiturner.com

Omar Tyree: www.omartyree.com

KaShamba Williams: www.precioustymes.com

Teri Woods: www.teriwoodspublishing.com

WORKS CITED

Aiex, Nola Kortner. 1993. *Bibliotherapy.* Eric Digest 82 (1993) www.eric.ed.gov/ PDFS/ED357333.pdf.

Alessio, Amy. 2004. Respect for the future: Making space for older teens. In *Serving older teens,* edited by Sheila B. Anderson Mikkelson, 87–102. Westport, CT: Libraries Unlimited.

Anderson, Elijah. 1999. *Code of the street: Decency, violence and the moral life of the inner-city.* New York: W. W. Norton.

Anderson, Elijah, and Cornel West. 2009. *Against the wall: Poor, young, black, and male (The city in the twenty-first century).* Philadelphia: University of Pennsylvania Press.

Appleyard, J. A. 1991. *Becoming a reader: The experience of fiction from childhood to adulthood.* Cambridge: Cambridge University Press.

Bartlett, Lesley, and Dorothy Holland. 2002. Theorizing the space of literacy practices. *Ways of Knowing Journal* 2, no. 1: 10–22.

Barton, David, and Mary Hamilton. 1998. *Local literacies: Reading and writing in one community.* New York: Routledge.

Bottigheimer, Ruth B. 2009. *Fairy tales: A new history.* Albany: State University of New York Press.

Bourgois, Philippe. 2002. *In search of respect: Selling crack in El Barrio.* Cambridge: Cambridge University Press.

Bourgois, Philippe. 2009. *Righteous dopefiend.* California Series in Public Anthropology. Berkeley: University of California Press.

Brooks, Wanda, and Linda Savage. 2009. Critiques and controversies of street literature. *ALAN Review* 36, no. 2: 48–55. http://scholar.lib.vt.edu/ejournals/ ALAN/v36n2/pdf/brooks.pdf.

Bruner, Jerome. 1986. *Actual minds, possible worlds.* Cambridge, MA: Harvard University Press.

Buvala, K. Sean. 2007. (1 + 2) < 3: The presence of the number 3 in folktales. Storyteller.net. July 24. www.storyteller.net/articles/222.

Campbell, Donna M. 2010. Naturalism in American literature. *Literary movements.* July 28. Department of English, Washington State University. www.wsu .edu/~campbelld/amlit/natural.htm.

Chance, Rosemary. 2008. *Young adult literature in action: A librarian's guide.* Santa Barbara, CA: Libraries Unlimited.

Chiles, N. 2006. Their eyes were reading smut. *New York Times.* Op-ed. January 4. www.nytimes.com/2006/01/04/opinion/04chiles.html?_r=1.

Citron, M. 1998. *Home movies and other necessary fictions.* Minneapolis: University of Minnesota Press.

Clark Cox, Ruth. 2008. Older teens are serious about their series: Forensic mysteries, graphic novels, horror, supernatural, and chick lit series. *Library Media Connection* 27, no. 3: 22–23.

Cochran-Smith, Marilyn, and Susan L. Lytle. 2009. *Inquiry as stance: Practitioner research in the next generation.* New York: Teachers College Press.

Compton-Lilly, Catherine. 2007. *(Re)reading families: The literate lives of urban children, four years later.* New York: Teachers College Press.

Dash, Leon. 1997. *Rosa Lee: A mother and her family in urban America.* New York: Plume.

Delpit, Lisa. 2006. *Other people's children: Cultural conflict in the classroom.* Rev. ed. New York: New Press.

Dimitriadis, George. 2003. *Friendship, cliques, and gangs: Young black men coming of age in urban America.* New York: Teachers College Press.

Doyle, Miranda. 2005. Sex, drugs, and drama: More books like *The Coldest Winter Ever. Voice of Youth Advocates* 28, no. 3: 190–93.

Fine, Michelle, and Lois Weis. 1998. *The unknown city: The lives of poor and working-class young adults.* Boston: Beacon Press.

Gorman, Michele, and Tricia Suellentrop. 2009. *Connecting young adults and libraries: A how-to-do-it manual.* 4th ed. New York: Neal-Schuman.

Hua, Anh. 2006. Memory and cultural trauma: Women of color in literature and film. Ph.D. dissertation, York University, Ontario.

Iser, Wolfgang. 1978. *The act of reading: A theory of aesthetic response.* Baltimore: John Hopkins University Press.

Jones, Gerald Everett. (2010). *Boychick lit.* Blog. www.boychiklit.com.

Katterjohn, Anna. 2010. Top twenty holds from Gary (IN) Public Library: From Sapphire to Usher, with adult, teen, and kids books and DVDs between. May 20. *Library Journal.* www.libraryjournal.com/lj/home/884038–264/top_twenty_holds_from_gary.html.csp.

Landay, Eileen. 2004. Performance as the foundation for a secondary school literacy program: A Bakhtinian perspective. In *Language, literacy and learning: Bakhtinian perspectives,* edited by Arnetha F. Ball and Sarah Warshauer Freedman. Cambridge: Cambridge University Press.

Lavenne, Francois-Xavier, Virginie Renard, and Francois Tollet. 2005. Fiction, between inner life and collective memory: A methodological reflection. *New Arcadia Review* 3. www.bc.edu/publications/newarcadia/archives/3.

Leadbeater, Bonnie J. Ross, and Niobe Way. 2007. *Urban girls revisited: Building strength.* New York: New York University Press.

Long, Elizabeth. 2003. *Book clubs: Women and the uses of reading in everyday life.* Chicago: University of Chicago Press.

Marshall, Elizabeth, Jeanine Staples, and Simone Gibson. 2009. Ghetto fabulous: Reading representations of black adolescent femininity in contemporary urban street fiction. *Journal of Adolescent and Adult Literacy 53,* no. 1: 28–36.

McFadden, Bernice L. 2010. Black writers in a ghetto of the publishing industry's making. *Washington Post,* June 26. www.washingtonpost.com/wp-dyn/content/article/2010/06/25/AR2010062504125.html.

McMillan, Terry. 2007. Subject: Emailing: Ray-J tell all memoir "Sex Machine" in the works. [public email correspondence]. October 3. Posted October 9, 2007, as From the desk of Terry McMillan. *Angeleque: Stories of seduction, passion, impulse and love.* http://angelequeford.com/2007/10/09/from-the-desk-of-terry-mcmillan/.

Moje, Elizabeth. 2000. "To be part of the story": The literacy practices of gangsta adolescents. *Teachers College Record* 3: 651–90.

Morris, Vanessa J. 2007. Inner-city teens do read: Their lives represented in urban street fiction. Paper presented at Beyond the Book: Contemporary Cultures of Reading, August 31–September 3, University of Birmingham. http://jahreinaresearch.info/urbanfiction/Inner%20City%20Teens%20Do%20Read.rtf.

Morris, Vanessa J., Denise E. Agosto, Sandra Hughes-Hassell, and Darren T. Cottman. 2006. Street lit: Flying off teen bookshelves in Philadelphia public libraries. *Journal of Young Adult Library Services* 5, no. 1: 16–23.

Newman, Katherine S. 1999. *No shame in my game: The working poor in the inner city.* New York: Alfred A. Knopf.

Nix, Taylor. 2009. Ashley and JaQuavis crack New York Times bestsellers list. *Urban Book Source: Your Online Authority for Urban Literature.* December. http://theubs.com/features/ashley-jaquavis.php?comments_page=6.

Owens, Lily, ed. 1981. *The complete Brothers Grimm fairy tales.* New York: Avenel/Crown.

Pernice, Ronda Racha. 2010. Black books are bigger than "ghetto lit." *Grio.* September 23. www.thegrio.com/entertainment/why-blacks-should-care-about-the-book-industrys-future.php.

Precious—The Response. 2009. *Street Literature* (blog). December 14. www.streetliterature.blogspot.com.

Radway, Janice. 1991. *Reading the romance: Women, patriarchy, and popular literature.* 2nd ed. London: Verso Press.

Rosenblatt, Louise. 1983. *Literature as exploration.* New York: Noble.

Shepard, Leslie. 1973. *The history of street literature: The story of broadside ballads, chapbooks, proclamations, news-sheets, election bills, tracts, pamphlets, cocks, catchpennies, and other ephemera.* Detroit: Singing Tree Press.

Shipler, David K. 2005. *The working poor: Invisible in America.* New York: Vintage.

Simon, David, and Edward Burns. 1997. *The corner: A year in the life of an inner city neighborhood.* New York: Broadway.

Stallman, Robert Wooster. 1955. Stephen Crane's revision of Maggie: A girl of the streets. *American Literature* 26, no. 4: 528–36. Durham, NC: Duke University Press.

Stringer, Lee. 2010. *Grand Central winter: Stories from the street.* New York: Seven Stories.

Sumara, Dennis. 1996. *Private readings in public: Schooling the literary imagination.* New York: Peter Lang.

Sweeney, Megan. 2010. *Reading is my window: Books and the art of reading in women's prisons.* Chapel Hill: University of North Carolina Press.

"thyung." 2005. *Urban Dictionary.* www.urbandictionary.com/authorphp?author=thyung.

Venkatesh, Sudhir. 2008. *Gang leader for a day: A rogue sociologist takes to the streets.* New York: Penguin.

Venkatesh, Sudhir A. 2006. *Off the books: The underground economy of the urban poor.* Cambridge, MA: Harvard University Press.

Warner, Judith. 2007. A warm welcome for "dad lit." *New York Times.* May 17. *Opinionator* blog. http://opinionator.blogs.nytimes.com/2007/05/17/a-warm-welcome-for-dad-lit/?apage=3.

Williams, Terry. 1993. *Crackhouse: Notes from the end of the line.* New York: Penguin.

Wilson, William Julius. 2009. *More than just race: Being black and poor in the inner city.* New York: W. W. Norton.

Worth, Robert R. 2002. Claude Brown, manchild of the promised land, dies at 64. *RaceMatters.org.* February 6. www.racematters.org/manchildinthepromisedland.htm.

Zernike, Kate. 2004. Oh, to write a "Bridget Jones" for men: A guy can dream. *New York Times.* February 22. www.nytimes.com/2004/02/22/style/oh-to-write-a-bridget-jones-for-men-a-guy-can-dream.html.

Zimmer, Melanie. 2002. Common symbols of transformation in fairy lore, legend, and biblical stories. Storyteller.net. www.storyteller.net/articles/68.

LITERATURE CITED

CANONICAL (FICTION)

Cahan, Abraham. [1896] 1970. *Yekl: A Tale of the New York Ghetto.* New York: Dover.

Crane, Stephen. [1893] 1986. *Maggie: A Girl of the Streets—A Story of New York.* New York: Bantam.

Crane, Stephen. [1895] 2000. *The Red Badge of Courage.* New York: Modern Library.

Defoe, Daniel. [1722] 1989. *The Fortunes and Misfortunes of the Famous Moll Flanders.* New York: Bantam.

Dickens, Charles. [1838] 1994. *Oliver Twist.* New York: Penguin.

Dickens, Charles. [1859-] 2003. *A Tale of Two Cities.* New York: Penguin.

Dunbar, Paul Laurence. [1902] 2011. *The Sport of the Gods.* New York: Signet.

Zangwill, Israel. [1892] 1998. *Children of the Ghetto: A Study of a Peculiar People.* Detroit: Wayne State University Press.

PIONEERING CLASSICS

Brown, Claude. 1965. *Manchild of the Promised Land.* New York: Macmillan.

Goines, Donald. 1974. *Daddy Cool.* Los Angeles: Holloway House.

Goines, Donald. 1971. *Dopefiend.* Los Angeles: Holloway House.

Himes, Chester. 1960. *All Shot Up.* New York: Berkley.

Himes, Chester. 1959. *Real Cool Killers.* New York: Avon.

Petry, Ann. 1946. *The Street.* Boston: Houghton Mifflin.

Puzo, Mario. 1965. *The Fortunate Pilgrim.* New York: Atheneum.

Puzo, Mario. 1969. *The Godfather.* New York: Putnam.

Slim, Iceberg. 1969. *Pimp: The Story of My Life.* Los Angeles: Holloway House.

Thomas, Piri. 1967. *Down These Mean Streets.* New York: Alfred A. Knopf.

Wright, Richard. 1940. *Native Son.* New York: Harper and Brothers.

X, Malcolm, and Alex Haley. 1965. *The Autobiography of Malcolm X.* New York: Grove Press.

CONTEMPORARY CLASSICS

Aaron, Relentless. 2007. *Push.* New York: St. Martin's.

Brown, Tracy. 2003. *Black: A Street Tale.* Columbus, OH: Triple Crown.

Clark, Wahida. 2004. *Thugs and the Women Who Love Them.* New York: Dafina.

Holmes, Shannon. 2001. *B-More Careful: A Novel.* New York: Teri Woods Publishing.

K'wan. 2005. *Hoodlum: A Novel.* New York: St. Martin's Griffin.

Sapphire. 1996. *Push.* New York: Alfred A. Knopf.

Slim, Iceberg. 1998. *Doomfox.* New York: Grove/Atlantic.

Souljah, Sister. 1999. *The Coldest Winter Ever.* New York: Atria.

Souljah, Sister. 2008. *Midnight: A Gangster Love Story.* New York: Atria.

Stringer, Vickie. 2002. *Let That Be the Reason.* Columbus, OH: Triple Crown.

Turner, Nikki. 2003. *A Hustler's Wife.* Columbus, OH: Triple Crown.

Tyree, Omar. 2000. *Flyy Girl.* New York: Simon and Schuster.

Woods, Teri. 1999. *True to the Game.* New York: Teri Woods Publishing.

CONTEMPORARY

Artemis, Black. 2006. *Burn.* New York: Penguin.

Artemis, Black. 2004. *Explicit Content.* New York: Penguin.

Ashley and JaQuavis. 2008. *The Cartel—1.* New York: Urban Books.

Ashley and JaQuavis. 2009. *The Cartel—2: Talk of the Murda Mamas.* New York: Urban Books.

Ashley and JaQuavis. 2010. *The Cartel—3: The Last Chapter.* New York: Urban Books.

Ashley and JaQuavis. 2005. *Diary of a Street Diva.* New York: Urban Books.

Brown, Tracy. 2005. *Criminal Minded.* New York: St. Martin's Griffin.

Brown, Tracy. 2007. *White Lines: A Novel.* New York: St. Martin's Griffin.

Cardona, Deborah (Sexy). 2007. *A Better Touch.* New York: Déjà Vu Publications.

Cardona, Deborah (Sexy). 2008. *Chained.* New York: Déjà Vu Publications.

Cardona, Deborah (Sexy). 2007. *A Gentleman's Sport.* New York: Déjà Vu Publications.

Cardona, Deborah (Sexy). 2007. *Two Fold.* New York: Déjà Vu Publications.

Carter, Quentin. 2005. *Hoodwinked.* Columbus, OH: Triple Crown.

Clark, Wahida. 2010. *The Golden Hustla.* New York: Grand Central.

Coleman, Darren. 2004. *Before I Let Go.* New York: Harper.

Coleman, Darren. 2007. *A Taste of Honey.* New York: Harper.

Ervin, Keisha. 2004. *Chyna Black.* Columbus, OH: Triple Crown.

Ervin, Keisha. 2006. *Hold U Down*. Columbus, OH: Triple Crown.

Ervin, Keisha. 2010. *Material Girl*. New York: Urban Books.

Ervin, Keisha. 2004. *Mina's Joint*. Columbus, OH: Triple Crown.

Frisby, Mister Mann. 2005. *Wifebeater*. New York: Riverhead Trade.

Gray, Erick S., and Mark Anthony. 2009. *The Streets of New York*, vol. 3. New York: Augustus.

Gray, Erick S., Anthony Whyte, and Mark Anthony. 2009. *The Streets of New York*, vol. 2. New York: Augustus.

Gray, Erick S., Mark Anthony, and Anthony Whyte. 2009. *The Streets of New York*, vol. 1. New York: Augustus.

Hawthorne, Tash. 2009. *Karma with a Vengeance*. East Orange, NJ: Wahida Clark Presents.

Holmes, Shannon. 2007. *Dirty Game*. New York: St. Martin's Griffin.

Holmes, Shannon. 2005. *Never Go Home Again: A Novel*. New York: Atria.

Jones, Solomon. 2003. *The Bridge: A Novel*. New York: Minotaur.

Jones, Solomon. 2007. *C.R.E.A.M.* New York: St. Martin's Griffin.

Jones, Solomon. 2001. *Pipe Dreams: A Novel*. New York: Villard/Strivers Row.

Jones, Solomon. 2005. *Ride or Die*. New York: Minotaur.

King, Joy. 2008. *Stackin' Paper*. Collierville, TN: A King Production.

K'wan. 2002. *Gangsta*. New York: St. Martin's Griffin.

K'wan. 2006. *Hood Rat: A Novel*. New York: St. Martin's Griffin.

K'wan. 2003. *Road Dawgz*. Columbus, OH: Triple Crown.

K'wan. 2009. *Section 8: A Hood Rat Novel*. New York: St. Martin's Griffin.

K'wan. 2004. *Street Dreams*. New York: St. Martin's Griffin.

Little, Terra. 2009. *Where There's Smoke*. New York: Urban Books.

Little, Terra. 2010. *Where There's Smoke 2*. New York: Urban Books.

Love, J. 2010. *The Game Don't Wait*. Los Angeles: Keep It Pushin' Productions.

Love, J. 2000. *Heavy in the Game*. Los Angeles: Keep It Pushin' Productions.

Noire. 2006. *Thug-a-Licious*. New York: One World/Ballantine.

Quinonez, Ernesto. 2000. *Bodega Dreams: A Novel*. New York: Vintage Contemporaries.

Rivera, Jeff. 2008. *Forever My Lady*. New York: Grand Central.

Robbins, Will. 2009. *ICE*. Columbus, OH: Triple Crown.

Serrano, Daniel. 2008. *Gunmetal Black*. New York: Grand Central.

Shakur, Sanyika. 2009. *T.H.U.G. L.I.F.E.* New York: Grove Press.

Stringer, Vickie. 2004. *Imagine This*. Columbus, OH: Triple Crown.

Sullivan, Leo. 2006. *Life*. Columbus, OH: Triple Crown.

Teague, Kwame. 2007. *Dutch III—The Finale*. New York: Teri Woods Publishing.

Teague, Kwame (Dutch). 2009. *Dynasty.* Washington, DC: DC Bookdiva.

Teague, Kwame (Dutch). 2008. *Thug Politics.* Washington, DC: DC Bookdiva.

Turner, Nikki. 2003. *A Project Chick.* Columbus, OH: Triple Crown.

Tyree, Omar. 2005. *Boss Lady.* New York: Simon and Schuster.

Tyree, Omar. 2001. *For the Love of Money.* New York: Simon and Schuster.

Williams, Brittani. 2010. *Black Diamond.* New York: Urban Books.

Williams, KaShamba. 2003. *Blinded: An Urban Tale!* Columbus, OH: Triple Crown.

Williams, KaShamba. 2005. *Driven: When You Can't Take Anything Else.* New York: Urban Books.

Williams, KaShamba. 2004. *Grimey: The Sequel to Blinded.* Columbus, OH: Triple Crown.

Woods, Teri. 2004. *Dutch.* New York: Teri Woods Publishing.

Woods, Teri. 2003. *Dutch: The First of a Trilogy.* New York: Teri Woods Publishing.

Woods, Teri. 2005. *Dutch II—Angel's Revenge.* New York: Teri Woods Publishing.

Woods, Teri. 2011. *Dutch III—International Gangster.* New York: Teri Woods Publishing.

Woods, Teri. 2007. *True to the Game II: Gena.* New York: Teri Woods Publishing.

Woods, Teri. 2008. *True to the Game III: Quadir.* New York: Teri Woods Publishing.

CONTEMPORARY SERIES

Around the Way Girls. Various authors. New York: Urban Books.

2007. La Jill Hunt and Angel Hunter. Volume 1.

2007. La Jill Hunt and Thomas Long. Volume 2.

2007. Pat Tucker, Alisha Yvonne, and Thomas Long. Volume 3.

2007. Roy Glenn, La Jill Hunt, and Thomas Long. Volume 4.

2008. Tysha, Mark Anthony, and Erick S. Gray. Volume 5.

2009. Mark Anthony, Meisha Camm, and B.L.U.N.T. Volume 6.

2010. Chunichi, Karen Williams, and B.L.U.N.T. Volume 7.

2011. Tina McKinney, B.L.U.N.T., and Meisha Camm Volume 8.

Bentley Manor Tales. Meesha Mink and De'nesha Diamond. New York: Touchstone.

2008. *Desperate Hoodwives: An Urban Tale.*

2008. *Shameless Hoodwives: A Bentley Manor Tale.*

2009. *Hood Life: A Bentley Manor Tale.*

Bitch. Deja King. Columbus, OH: Triple Crown.

2004. *Bitch.* Part 1.

2007. *Bitch, Reloaded.* Part 2.

2008. *The Bitch Is Back.* Part 3.

2008. *Queen Bitch.* Part 4. Collierville, TN: A King Production.

2009. *Last Bitch Standing, Part 5: A Novel.* Collierville, TN: A King Production.

Dirty Red. Vickie Stringer. New York: Atria.

2006. *Dirty Red.*

2008. *Still Dirty: A Novel.*

2010. *Dirtier Than Ever: A Novel.*

Flint. Treasure Hernandez. New York: Urban Books.

2008. *Choosing Sides.* Book 1.

2008. *Working Girls.* Book 2.

2008. *Back to the Streets.* Book 3.

2008. *Resurrection.* Book 4.

2009. *Back to the Hood.* Book 5.

2009. *A King Is Born.* Book 6.

2010. *The Finale.* Book 7.

Gangster Girl. Chunichi. New York: Urban Books.

2004. *A Gangster's Girl.* Part 1.

2005. *Married to the Game.* Part 2.

2006. *The Naked Truth.* Part 3.

2007. *A Gangster's Girl Saga* (parts 1–3 compilation).

2007. *The Return of a Gangster's Girl.* Part 4.

Girls from da Hood. Various authors. New York: Urban Books.

2004. Nikki Turner, Chunichi, and Roy Glenn. Volume 1.

2005. KaShamba Williams, Joy, and Nikki Turner. Volume 2.

2006. KaShamba Williams, Mark Anthony, and Madame K. Volume 3.

2008. Ashley and JaQuavis and Ayana Ellis.   Volume 4.

2009. Keisha Ervin, Brenda Hamilton, and Ed McNair. Volume 5.

2011. Ashley and JaQuavis and Amaleka McCall. Volume 6.

In My Hood. Endy. New York: Melodrama.

2007. *In My Hood, 1.*

2008. *In My Hood, 2.*

2009. *In My Hood, 3.*

Wifey. Kiki Swinson. Bellport, NY: Melodrama.

2004.*Wifey.* Part 1.

2005. *I'm Still Wifey.* Part 2.

2007. *Life after Wifey.* Part 3.

2008. *Still Wifey Material.* Part 4.

2010. *Wife for Life.* Part 5.

2011. *Wifey Extraordinaire.* Part 6. Virginia Beach, VA: K. S. Publications.

THUG-LOVE FICTION SERIES

Clark, Wahida. 2004. *Thugs and the Women Who Love Them.* New York: Dafina.

Clark, Wahida. 2006. *Every Thug Needs a Lady.* New York: Dafina.

Clark, Wahida. 2008. *Thug Matrimony.* New York: Dafina.

Clark, Wahida. 2009. *Thug Lovin'.* New York: Grand Central.

GLBTQ

Britt, A. C. 2007. *London Reign.* New York: GhettoHeat.

Brown, Laurinda D. 2007. *Strapped.* New York: Urban Books.

Collins, D. L. 2007. *A Stud's Love: A Lesbian Drama.* Bloomington, IN: iUniverse.

Hall, Reginald L. 2007. *In Love with a Thug.* New York: Strebor.

Jackson, Missy. 2009. *Cheetah: Always Be Ahead of the Hustle.* East Orange, NJ: Wahida Clark Presents.

Kahari, Asante. 2004. *Homo Thug.* New York: Gotham City.

Kahari, Asante. 2009. *Homo Thug 2.* New York: Harlem Book Center.

Meadows, Damon, and Jason Poole. 2006. *Convict's Candy.* New York: GhettoHeat.

N'Tyse. 2007. *My Secrets Your Lies.* Dallas: A Million Thoughts.

Nero, Clarence. 2006. *Three Sides to Every Story: A Novel.* New York: Harlem Moon.

Pope, M. T. 2009. *Both Sides of the Fence.* New York: Urban Books.

Pope, M. T. 2010. *Both Sides of the Fence 2.* New York: Urban Books.

Racheal, Christine. 2010. *Trickery.* Columbus, OH: Triple Crown.

Sidi. 2006. *The Lesbian's Wife.* New York: Harlem Book Center.

Vernon, Dwayne. 2010. *Roman.* Baltimore: Norcarjo.

TEEN AND TWEEN FICTION

Booth, Coe. 2008. *Kendra.* New York: Push.

Booth, Coe. 2006. *Tyrell.* New York: Push.

Buckhanon, Kalisha. 2005. *Upstate.* New York: St. Martin's Press.

Dupree, Kia. 2010. *Damaged.* New York: Grand Central.

Flake, Sharon. 2005. *Bang!* New York: Hyperion/Jump at the Sun.

Flake, Sharon. 2003. *Begging for Change.* New York: Hyperion/Jump at the Sun.

Flake, Sharon. 2001. *Money Hungry.* New York: Hyperion/Jump at the Sun.

Flake, Sharon. 1998. *The Skin I'm In.* New York: Hyperion/Jump at the Sun.

Flake, Sharon. 2004. *Who Am I without Him?* New York: Hyperion/Jump at the Sun.

Flake, Sharon. 2010. *You Don't Even Know My Name: Stories and Poems about Boys.* New York: Hyperion/Jump at the Sun.

Frost, Helen. 2007. *Keesha's House.* New York: Farrar, Straus, and Giroux.

McDonald, Janet. 2004. *Brother Hood.* New York: Farrar, Straus, and Giroux.

McDonald, Janet. 2006. *Chill Wind.* New York: Farrar, Straus, and Giroux.

McDonald, Janet. 2000. *Project Girl.* Berkeley: University of California Press.

McDonald, Janet. 2003. *Twists and Turns.* New York: Farrar, Straus, and Giroux.

Myers, Walter Dean. 1999. *Monster.* New York: Amistad.

Myers, Walter Dean. 2009. *Dopesick.* New York: Amistad.

Myers, Walter Dean. 2006. *Street Love.* New York: Amistad.

Myers, Walter Dean, and Christopher Myers. 2005. *Autobiography of My Dead Brother.* New York: Amistad.

TEEN AND TWEEN SERIES

Baby Girl Drama. Babygirl Daniels. New York: Urban Books.

2009. *16 on the Block.* Volume 1.

2009. *16½ on the Block.* Volume 2.

2009. *Sister Sister.* Volume 3.

2009. *Glitter.* Volume 4.

Beta Gamma Pi. Stephanie Perry Moore. Chicago: Moody Press.

2009. *Work What You Got.* Book 1.

2009. *The Way We Roll.* Book 2.

2009. *Act Like You Know.* Book 3.

2010. *Got It Going On.* Book 4.

2010. *Get What You Give.* Book 5.

Bluford High. Various authors. West Berlin, NJ: Townsend Press/Scholastic.

2001. Anne Schraff. *Lost and Found.* Volume 1.

2001. Anne Schraff and Paul Langan. *A Matter of Trust.* Volume 2.

2001. Anne Schraff. *Secrets in the Shadows.* Volume 3.

2001. Paul Langan. *Someone to Love Me.* Volume 4.

2002. Paul Langan. *The Bully.* Volume 5.

2002. Paul Langan. *The Gun.* Volume 6.

2002. Paul Langan and Anne Schraff. *Until We Meet Again.* Volume 7.

2004. Paul Langan and D. M. Blackwell. *Blood Is Thicker.* Volume 8.

2004. Paul Langan and Ben Alirez. *Brothers in Arms.* Volume 9.

2004. Paul Langan. *Summer of Secrets.* Volume 10.

2007. Paul Langan. *The Fallen.* Volume 11.

2007. Paul Langan. *Shattered.* Volume 12.

2007. John Langan and Paul Langan. *Search for Safety.* Volume 13.

2008. Peggy Kern and Paul Langan. *No Way Out.* Volume 14.

2008. Paul Langan. 2008. *Schooled.* Volume 15.

Carmen Browne. Stephanie Perry Moore. Chicago: Moody.

2005. *True Friends.* Book 1.

2005. *Sweet Honesty.* Book 2.

2006. *Golden Spirit.* Book 3.

2006. *Perfect Joy.* Book 4.

2007. *Happy Princess.* Book 5.

Del Rio Bay Clique. Paula Chase Hyman. New York: Dafina.

2007. *Don't Get It Twisted.*

2008. *That's What's Up!*

2008. *Who You Wit'?*

2009. *Flipping the Script.*

Denim Diaries. Darrien Lee. New York: Urban Books.

2008. *16 Going on 21.* Volume 1.

2009. *Grown in Sixty Seconds.* Volume 2.

2009. *Queen of the Yard.* Volume 3.

2009. *Broken Promises.* Volume 4.

2010. *Raising Kane.* Volume 5.

Divas. Victoria Christopher Murray. New York: Pocket Books.

2008. *Diamond.* Book 1.

2008. *India.* Book 2.

2009. *Veronique.* Book 3.

2009. *Aaliyah.* Book 4.

Divine. Jacquelin Thomas. New York: Pocket Books.

2006. *Simply Divine, #1.*

2007. *Divine Confidential, #2.*

2007. *Divine Secrets, #3.*

2008. *Divine Match-Up, #4.*

Divine and Friends. Jacquelin Thomas. New York: Pocket Books.

2009. *It's a Curl Thing, #1.*

2010. *Split Ends, #2.*

Drama High. L. Divine. New York: Dafina.

2006. *The Fight.* Volume 1.

2006. *Second Chance.* Volume 2.

2007. *Jayd's Legacy.* Volume 3.

2008. *Frenemies.* Volume 4.

2008. *Lady J.* Volume 5.

2008. *Courtin' Jayd.* Volume 6.

2009. *Hustlin'.* Volume 7.

2009. *Keep It Movin'.* Volume 8.

2009. *Holidaze.* Volume 9.

2010. *Culture Clash.* Volume 10.

2010. *Cold as Ice.* Volume 11.

2010. *Pushin'.* Volume 12.

2011. *The Meltdown.* Volume 13.

Good Girlz. ReShonda Tate Billingsley. New York: Pocket Books.

2006. *Nothing but Drama.* Book 1.

2007. *Blessings in Disguise.* Book 2.

2007. *With Friends Like These.* Book 3.

2008. *Getting Even.* Book 4.

2008. *Fair Weather Friends.* Book 5.

2009. *Friends 'til the End*. Book 6.

2010. *Caught Up in the Drama*. Book 7.

Kimani Tru. Various authors. New York: Kimani.

2007. Joyce E. Davis. *Can't Stop the Shine*. Book 1.

2007. Earl Sewell. *Keysha's Drama*. Book 2.

2007. Chandra Sparks Taylor. *Spin It Like That*. Book 3.

2007. Cassandra Carter. *Fast Life*. Book 4.

2007. Cecil Cross. *First Semester*. Book 5.

2007. Felicia Pride. *Hallway Diaries*. Book 6.

2007. Scott Nyomi. *Gettin' Hooked*. Book 7.

2007. Monica McKayhan. *Trouble Follows*. Book 8.

2008. Dona Salkar. *How to Salsa in a Sari*. Book 9.

2008. Hayden. *A Matter of Attitude*. Book 10.

2008. Cassandra Carter. *16 Isn't Always Sweet*. Book 11.

2008. Celeste O. Norfleet. *She Said, She Said*. Book 12.

2008. Earl Sewell. *If I Were Your Boyfriend*. Book 13.

2008. Philip Thomas Duck. *Dirty Jersey*. Book 14.

2008. Chandra Sparks Taylor. *The Pledge*. Book 15.

2008. Monica McKayhan. *Jaded*. Book 16.

2009. Beverly Jenkins. *Belle*. Book 17.

2009. Celeste O. Norfleet. *Fast Forward*. Book 18.

2009. Earl Sewell. *Lesson Learned*. Book 19.

2009. Kendra Lee. *Keeping Secrets*. Book 20.

2009. Monica McKayhan. *Deal with It*. Book 21.

2009. Philip Thomas Duck. *Dirty South*. Book 22.

2009. Felicia Pride. *Patterson Heights*. Book 23.

2009. Earl Sewell. *Decision Time*. Book 24.

2010. Cecil Cross. *Next Semester*. Book 25.

2010. Simone Bryant. *Fabulous*. Book 26.

2010. Chandra Sparks Taylor. *The Promise*. Book 27.

2010. Monica McKayhan. *Step Up*. Book 28.

2010. Arthur Artist. *Manifest*. Book 29.

2010. Earl Sewell. *Myself and I*. Book 30.

2011. Simone Bryant. *Famous*. Book 31.

Payton Skky. Stephanie Perry Moore. Chicago: Moody.

2000. *Staying Pure, 1.*

2000. *Sober Faith, 2.*

2001. *Saved Race, 3.*

2001. *Sweetest Gift, 4.*

2002. *Surrendered Heart, 5.*

Perry Skky, Jr. Stephanie Perry Moore. Chicago: Moody.

2007. *Prime Choice, 1.*

2007. *Pressing Hard, 2.*

2007. *Problem Solved, 3.*

2008. *Prayed Up, 4.*

2008. *Promise Kept, 5.*

Platinum Teen. Various authors. Bear, DE: Precioustymes Entertainment.

2005. Precious and KaShamba Williams. *Dymond in the Rough.* Book 1.

2005. Precious and Juwell. *The Absolute Truth.* Book 2.

2006. Precious and Juwell. *Runaway.* Book 3.

2008. Precious and KaShamba Williams. *Best Kept Secret.* Book 4.

Ni Ni Simone. Ni Ni Simone. New York: Dafina.

2008. *Shortie Like Mine.* Book 1.

2008. *If I Was Your Girl.* Book 2.

2008. *A Girl Like Me.* Book 3.

2010. *Teen Age Love Affair.* Book 4.

Yasmin Peace. Stephanie Perry Moore. Chicago: Moody.

2009. *Finding Your Faith.* Book 1.

2009. *Believing in Hope.* Book 2.

2009. *Experiencing the Joy.* Book 3.

2009. *Learning to Love.* Book 4.

2010. *Enjoying True Peace.* Book 5.

PICTURE BOOKS

Allen, Debbie, and Kadir Nelson. 2001. *Brothers of the Knight.* New York: Puffin.

Crews, Nina. 2003. *Neighborhood Mother Goose.* New York: Greenwillow.

Keats, Ezra Jack. 1969. *Goggles!* New York: Macmillan.

Keats, Ezra Jack. 1962. *The Snowy Day*. New York: Viking Juvenile.

Norman, Lissette, and Frank Morrison. 2006. *My Feet Are Laughing*. New York: Farrar, Straus, and Giroux.

Ringgold, Faith. 1996. *Tar Beach*. New York: Dragonfly.

Sendak, Maurice. 1993. *We Are All in the Dumps with Jack and Guy: Two Nursery Rhymes with Pictures*. New York: HarperCollins.

GRAPHIC NOVELS

Carey, Percy. 2008. *Sentences: The Life of M. F. Grimm*. Illustrations by Ronald Wimberly. New York: Vertigo and DC Comics.

David, Mark, and Mike Davis. 2007. Blokhedz, *Volume 1: Genesis*. New York: Pocket Books.

Eminem. 2004. *In My Skin: The Eminem Graphic*. London: Omnibus Press.

Goines, Donald. 2006. *Daddy Cool (Graphic)*. Los Angeles: Holloway House.

Hoke, Ahmed. 2003. *@large*. Los Angeles: Tokyopop.

Landowne, Youme, and Anthony Horton. 2008. *Pitch Black, Don't Be Skerd*. El Paso, TX: Cinco Puntos.

Wood, Brian. 2008. *Fight for Tomorrow*. New York: Vertigo.

NONFICTION (POETRY)

Brown, Jericho. 2008. *Please*. Kalamazoo, MI: New Issues Poetry and Prose.

Holter, Jessica. 2003. *Speak the Unspeakable*. Oakland, CA: GGB Literary Entertainment.

Medina, Tony, and Louis Reyes Rivera, eds. 2001. *Bum Rush the Page: A Def Poetry Slam*. Foreword by Sonia Sanchez. New York: Three Rivers.

Scott, Jill. 2005. *The Moments, the Minutes, the Hours: The Poetry of Jill Scott*. New York: St. Martin's Griffin.

Shakur, Tupac. 1999. *The Rose That Grew from Concrete*. New York: MTV/Pocket Books.

Smith, Patricia. 1998. *Close to Death: Poems*. Cambridge, MA: Zoland.

Williams, Saul. 2006. *The Dead Emcee Scrolls: The Lost Teachings of Hip Hop*. New York: MTV.

NONFICTION (BIOGRAPHIES AND MEMOIRS)

50 Cent, with Kris Ex. 2005. *From Pieces to Weight: Once upon a Time in Southside Queens*. New York: MTV.

Betts, R. Dwayne. 2009. *A Question of Freedom: A Memoir of Learning, Survival, and Coming of Age in Prison*. New York: Penguin/Avery.

Canada, Geoffrey. 1995. *Fish, Stick, Knife, Gun: A Personal History of Violence in America*. Boston: Beacon Press.

Davis, Sampson, George Jenkins, Rameck Hunt, and Sharon Draper. 2006. *We Beat the Street: How a Friendship Pact Led to Success*. New York: Puffin.

DMX, and Smokey D. Fontaine. 2003. *E.A.R.L.: The Autobiography of DMX*. New York: HarperCollins.

Jasper, Kenji. 2006. *The House on Childress Street: A Memoir*. New York: Harlem Moon.

Jones, LeAlan, and Lloyd Newman. 1998. *Our America: Life and Death on the Southside of Chicago*. New York: Scribner.

Kotlowitz, Alex. 1992. *There Are No Children Here: The Story of Two Boys Growing Up in the Other America*. New York: Anchor Books.

LeBlanc, Adrian Nicole. 2003. *Random Family: Love, Drugs, Trouble, and Coming of Age in the Bronx*. New York: Scribner.

McCall, Nathan. 1995. *Makes Me Wanna Holler: A Young Black Man in America*. New York: Vintage.

Morris, DeShaun "Jiwe." 2008. *War of the Bloods in My Veins: A Street Soldier's March toward Redemption*. New York: Scribner.

Pearson, Felicia "Snoop." 2007. *Grace after Midnight: A Memoir*. New York: Grand Central.

S., Tina, and Jamie Pastor Bolnick. 2000. *Living at the Edge of the World: A Teenager's Survival in the Tunnels of Grand Central Station*. New York: St. Martin's Press.

Sanchez, Ivan. 2008. *Next Stop: Growing Up Wild Style in the Bronx*. New York: Touchstone.

Sanchez, Reymundo. 2000. *My Bloody Life: The Making of a Latin King*. Chicago: Chicago Review Press.

Sanchez, Reymundo, and Sonia Rodriguez. 2008. *Lady Q: The Rise and Fall of a Latin Queen*. Chicago: Chicago Review Press.

Shakur, Sanyika. 2004. *Monster: The Autobiography of a L.A. Gang Member*. New York: Grove Press.

Souljah, Sister. 1995. *No Disrespect*. New York: Vintage.

Thomas-El, Salome, with Cecil Murphey. 2003. *I Choose to Stay: A Black Teacher Refuses to Desert the Inner City*. New York: Kensington.

Williams, Stanley Tookie. 2007. *Blue Rage, Black Redemption: A Memoir*. New York: Touchstone.

OTHER LITERATURE (NOT STREET LITERATURE) CITED

Bronte, Charlotte. [1847] 2006. *Jane Eyre*. New York: Penguin Classics.

Burch, Christian. 2006. *The Manny Files*. New York: Atheneum Books for Young Readers.

Bushnell, Candace. *Sex in the City.* New York: Atlantic Monthly Press.

Butler, Octavia. 1977. *Mind of My Mind.* New York: Doubleday.

Carlson, Lori Marie. 2005. *Red Hot Salsa: Bilingual Poems on Being Young and Latino in the United States.* New York: Henry Holt.

Carlson, Melody. 2000–2010. *Diary of a Teenage Girl.* Sister, OR: Multnomah.

Elliott, Zetta. 2010. *A Wish after Midnight.* Seattle: Amazon Encore.

Fielding, Helen. 1996. *Bridget Jones's Diary: A Novel.* London: Picador.

Fitzgerald, Scott. 1925. *The Great Gatsby.* New York: Scribner.

Hopkinson, Nalo. 1998. *Brown Girl in the Ring.* New York: Warner.

LaHaye, Tim, and Jerry B. Jenkins. 1995–2007. *Left Behind.* Carol Stream, IL: Tyndale House.

Marshall, Paule. 1959. *Brown-Girl, Brownstones.* New York: Feminist Press at City University of New York.

Mosley, Walter. 1997. *Always Outnumbered, Always Outgunned.* New York: W. W. Norton.

Naylor, Gloria. 1982. *Women of Brewster Place.* New York: Penguin.

Ruark, Robert Chester. 1965. *The Honey Badger.* New York: Fawcett.

Smith, Kyle. 2004. *Love Monkey.* New York: Morrow.

Von Ziegesar, Cecily. 2002–2009. *Gossip Girl.* Boston: Little, Brown.

Walker, Alice. 1982. *The Color Purple.* New York: Harcourt Brace Jovanovich.

INDEX

You may also be interested in

THE READERS' ADVISORY GUIDE TO GRAPHIC NOVELS
Francisca Goldsmith

"The American Library Association (ALA) adds another excellent and, in this case, much-needed volume to its readers' advisory library with this succinct guide . . . a valuable and quite readable resource that belongs in every library's professional collection."
—*VOYA*

PRINT ISBN: 978-0-8389-1008-5
136 PAGES / 6" x 9"

THE READERS' ADVISORY GUIDE TO MYSTERY, 2E
JOHN CHARLES, CANDACE CLARK, JOANNE HAMILTON-SELWAY, AND JOANNA MORRISON
ISBN: 978-0-8389-1113-6

THE READERS' ADVISORY GUIDE TO HORROR, 2E
BECKY SIEGEL SPRATFORD
ISBN: 978-0-8389-1112-9

THE READERS' ADVISORY HANDBOOK
EDITED BY JESSICA E. MOYER & KAITE MEDIATORE STOVER
ISBN: 978-0-8389-1042-9

FANG-TASTIC FICTION
PATRICIA O'BRIEN MATHEWS
ISBN: 978-0-8389-1073-3

THE READERS' ADVISORY GUIDE TO GENRE FICTION, 2E
JOYCE G. SARICKS
ISBN: 978-0-8389-0989-8

SERVING BOYS THROUGH READERS' ADVISORY
MICHAEL SULLIVAN
ISBN: 978-0-8389-1022-1

Order today at **alastore.ala.org** or **866-746-7252!**

ALA Store purchases fund advocacy, awareness, and accreditation programs for library professionals worldwide.